D1642596

There is no such thing as an ord[ ] unique story to tell as they stan[ ] past and daring to embrace the p[ ] rippling with the beauty of the extraordinary. We see [ ] Val's personal story. Yet this is not a book about an isolated individual; rather it is about how we go on becoming who we are in relationship with God and neighbour. These pages reveal a woman who has entered into the stories of those who so often remain hidden in the shadows, and amid the mess and brokenness of life Val has lived love and hope, and invited people to walk good new chapters in their own story. And at the heart of it all is the story of Jesus Christ, and the truth that crucifixion and resurrection dwell together. There is no such thing as an ordinary story.

Rt Revd Rachel Treweek, Bishop of Gloucester

Inspirational!

Rob Parsons, OBE, founder and chairman of Care for the Family

This is a book of miracles, and an astonishing witness to the love of Christ made incarnate in one woman's determination to bring dignity and healing to society's most marginalized and exploited women. To have known and worked with Val Jeal for a few years as a volunteer with One25 changed my life, but reading this I realize that I had barely scratched the surface of all there was to know and love. This is the story of a faithful disciple who has truly grasped 'how wide and long and high and deep is the love of Christ', in the midst of heartbreak and struggle, failure and desolation, but also with abundant joy, humour and hope.

Tina Beattie, Professor Emerita of
Catholic Studies, University of Roehampton

Back in the 1980s, along with my wife Margaret, I had the privilege of playing a small part in Val Jeal's story. Having given her life to Jesus during one of our services, she and her husband Cliff quickly became valued and much-loved members of our congregation in the St Paul's area of Bristol. Little did I realize back then, however, where Val's faith journey would take her or just how remarkable her story would turn out to be. She tells that story in this absorbing book. At times it will make you smile or even laugh out loud. At other times it will reduce you to tears. But always it will cause you to rejoice in what Val describes as God's 'enormous, generous, heartbreaking love' and what God can do with us and through us when we open ourselves up to that love.

Chick Yuill, speaker, writer, and presenter
for Premier Christian Radio

Be inspired by reading Val's story: the story of a woman who gave her heart to God, so he could work through her for over 30 years to bring love and transformation to female sex workers on the streets of Bristol. Be inspired by the stories she tells of pain, courage and hope, as she set up the trailblazing charity, One25, which helps Bristol's most marginalized women move from crisis and trauma to independence in the community. Be challenged by Val's statement that when God needs someone to go, let it be you!

Roger Allen, Together4Bristol / Churches
Together in Greater Bristol

Broken By Love

Transforming the lives of women on the streets of Bristol

Val Jeal
with Jude Simpson

Authentic

British Library Cataloguing in Publication Data
A catalogue record for this book is available from the British Library.
ISBN: 978-1-78893-286-8
978-1-78893-287-5 (e-book)

Cover design by Vivian Hanson de los Rios
Printed and bound by Bell & Bain Ltd, Glasgow, G46 7UQ

Some of the names in this book have been changed for anonymity.

For Hannah,
my lovely granddaughter,
with love

Foreword

To embark on reading this book is to journey with a woman who has abandoned herself to the radical guiding of God's Spirit. Val takes the reader into the brutal reality of life and death, joy and sorrow on the streets of St Paul's and neighbouring areas of Bristol.

This book is full of personal stories and encounters, of shared hopes and dreams, of human souls meeting on life's path. Val doesn't enter the world of poverty and prostitution, alcohol and drug dependency in order to 'fix' anyone. Rather she comes, with the fire of God burning in her heart, to love, to be alongside, to honour, to listen and to nurture and when possible, to offer opportunities.

These pages also include a number of disturbing facts and statistics which are an essential backdrop of the reality of those she meets and a challenge to the reader. It is not for the fainthearted.

Seeing Val in action is quite something! This unassuming woman has a huge heart of love and compassion for those on the margins of society. In addition, Val also possesses a godly fierceness that has seen her overcome the most unimaginable odds to bring her God-given visions to fruition and a courage she does not own or recognize. I remain in awe of all that Val has been able to bring about.

This is a deeply personal account of Val's own journey of faith and discipleship, and it is no easy path. Here we meet a woman who is not afraid to be vulnerable, be open to receive, be loved by those she serves and be hurt and even be broken. I can't help recalling the words of Teresa of Avila who said to God: 'If this is how you treat your friends, no wonder you have so few of them!'

I have had the great privilege of being a friend of Val since the early 1990s when I was inspired by her vision to provide a service for the women working in the street-based sex industry in the St Paul's area of Bristol. This was to become the One25 project which Val founded. In those early years we covered many miles in the van's outreach and were called 'angels of the night'! We have sat through hours of meetings, laughed, wept, and prayed with beautiful women who have been dealt the most brutal of life's cards; we have stood in court together, visited women in prison, at home, and in hospital, but we have celebrated with those who left the streets. We have attended far too many funerals.

In the years of our ongoing friendship, Val and I can also put on record plentiful supplies of cream teas shared together, pints of hot chocolate and copious amounts of cake!

It is thanks to Val that so many lives have been transformed through a number of projects she instigated. Although some of these projects like Naomi House very sadly did not continue, the lives that were radically changed and the babies enabled to stay with their mothers, bear a living witness to the efficacy of such a project and the desperate ongoing need for them.

One25 continues to reach out, support and empower women and is the thriving award-winning charity we still see today.

I close with the words of a young woman who left the streets and came to say thank you: 'you looked at me as if I was a human being when I had forgotten it myself'.

Sister Annaliese
Community of the Sisters of the Church

Contents

1

The End

How do I begin a book that I never wanted to write? A book that will bring up all kinds of painful emotions and memories, and break my heart all over again?

There have been many moments of joy, and even of triumph in my years of working with marginalized people. I have seen lives turned around, souls saved, people rescued from distress, addiction and poverty. But not all of them. And none of the joys came without me first experiencing loss, frustration, sadness and grief.

I grew to love and respect people whom the world had overlooked, given up on. Many times, I loved people until they died. God shared his loving, broken heart with me, and although that was a privilege, it was – and still is – a painful one.

Yet I believe the Holy Spirit is prompting me to write.

My name is Val Jeal. I have an Honorary Doctorate in Laws from the University of Bristol. I have an MBE for services to homeless people, which I received from the Queen at Buckingham Palace. I am the first woman ever to be granted the Freedom of the City of Bristol – which is a wonderful honour, and also means that I'm allowed to graze my sheep on Bristol common whenever I like!

My story and the work I began have been recognized as trailblazing – held up as a gold standard by many agencies throughout the UK and even beyond. But all these honours I accepted not for myself, but on behalf of the marginalized, powerless yet courageous women it has been my privilege to work with for the last thirty years.

Because what am I? I'm a woman who gave her heart to God, who made mistakes, who loved people the best she could, who tried to learn through everything she did, including the mistakes. I'm a woman who tried always to improve, who often succeeded and often failed. A woman who learned – the hard way – to always do things in God's strength, not my own. I'm a woman who did it because of a love God had put in her heart for men and women without power or influence in the world, who deserve to know and be changed by the power of Jesus.

This isn't an extraordinary tale of some incredible person – someone out of the ordinary with special gifts, or a one-in-a-million personality. No. This is me, Val, now aged 82, telling you that God is good, that the world is hurting, and that trying to give people the help they need is acutely painful, very costly, often disappointing, but always, always worthwhile.

This is me, Val, saying, when God needs someone to go – let it be you. Not because you're qualified, gifted, talented, or unique (although you probably are) but because God will do the work through you, if you let him – if you allow him to show you his love, both for you and the people around you: his enormous, generous, heart-breaking love.

Let me take you back to November 1995. It's a Tuesday morning. I'm at the Salvation Army Citadel, right in the heart of St Paul's, one of the poorest neighbourhoods of Bristol, in the south-west of England. It's a rather dilapidated, box-shaped building on the corner of Ashley Road and Brigstocke Road. On the other side of the street are the graffiti-daubed back garden gates of tall, Edwardian houses – built at the time when Bristol had a busy harbour and shipbuilding industries, was a famous railway terminus and an emerging aircraft industry hub.

In other, more fashionable areas of the city, houses like these are now selling for vast sums, popping up regularly on trendy Instagram feeds and Estate Agent Top Picks. Not here.

Within shouting distance of the Citadel, there's a halal butcher, a café serving Caribbean cuisine, an international mini-market, a vintage record shop, and some of the best – but always opinion-splitting – street art in Bristol. There are foodbanks, charity shops, boarded-up shops, hostels, and many different people going about their many different kinds of lives.

Back then, I was the manager for the Candle drop-in centre at the Citadel, and our Tuesday morning session was busy, with around fifty people having come off the streets to enjoy the hot drinks and sandwiches our volunteers offered them. Part of my job was just to keep abreast of it all – to keep an eye on everything that was going on.

I noticed a very chaotic female drug user we knew – her name was Jan – go into the toilet. I automatically started timing her. This was normal practice – to time people using the toilets – you wanted to make sure they were actually going to the toilet, not taking the opportunity to use drugs. After the standard ten minutes, Jan had not reappeared, so I tapped on the door and called out to her, asking if all was well. There was no reply.

I knocked again, a bit louder, and shouted again. Nothing. After a few more attempts, and no responses, I unlocked the door from the outside. There, to my horror, was Jan, slumped on the floor with her back against the toilet and her feet against the tiled wall. Blood was spurting out from an artery in her left foot. She had evidently tried to inject heroin and the needle had snapped, part of it still embedded in her foot.

She was conscious, and immediately became verbally aggressive, yelling at me for intruding on her, swearing and abusing me. Despite the injury, and all the blood, she got to her feet, pushed me aside, and stumbled out into the drop-in centre, where everyone suddenly fell silent.

I shouted for someone to ring for an ambulance and tried to reason with Jan, tried to get her to sit down, until the paramedics came. She was having none of it. Before any of us could stop her, she managed to get into the medical room – somehow the door had been left open by the cleaner after the morning clinic. Jan started wrecking the room – grabbing boxes and equipment off the shelves and throwing them on the floor, crashing into the chair and the desk.

I had difficulty getting her out. I didn't know what to do, I was exhausted and emotional. I didn't feel in control of the situation. She was pushing and shoving me as I tried to bring her back in the main room to stop the destruction. In my panic, I was also furious. How dare she abuse that space. I tried to stop her flailing arms, but she pushed me, kicked at me. Then she spat in my face.

I don't know if you know what it's like to be spat at. There's something horrible, really horrible about it. I was bruised from the kicking, I had her blood on my clothes and hands, but it was that spit on my face . . . I remember washing my face more than once before I went to report the incident to my manager, and tell him what a mess I'd made of it. I washed my face, over and over, but it felt like I couldn't get it clean.

The paramedics were amazing. They were familiar with Jan, of course. They managed eventually to get her into the ambulance, and took her to Bristol Royal Infirmary. It took four of us to clear up the centre afterwards.

I'm not starting with this story to show you what a hard time we had, or how extraordinary I am to face situations that many of you haven't had to face. I'm certainly not trying to make you feel like I was some sort of hero – as you can tell, I really wasn't. Actually, I was even less of a hero than I've so far let you see – but more of that later.

The reason I'm starting with this story is because this is the moment when I realized that I was absolutely, completely, utterly finished.

And so, in that topsy-turvy way that God seems to operate – this story, of me coming to the end of myself, is where everything began.

2

From Northumberland to Jerusalem . . . and Back

My own beginnings were fairly humble. On my mother's side, the background was one of poverty. Her father was a sailor who mysteriously disappeared while at sea, leaving his wife – my grandmother – a widow with three children. The eldest, at 5 years of age, was my mother. My grandmother was a woman of strength and determination, who was definitely not to be messed with! She held the family together and ensured that each of her three children were educated and had a future – my mother as an apprentice seamstress in Bristol, where they lived.

My mother became an accomplished seamstress, and also a strong woman. During my father's absence in the war, and later when he spent years in hospitals, Mum kept the family together and provided for my younger brother, Malcolm, and me. I was born in 1941 in Newbiggin-by-the-Sea, Northumberland. My father, having been a regular soldier, was called up at the beginning of the Second World War in 1939 and was posted to Northumberland. Because my parents had lost two babies before I was born, it was decided that Mum would move to Northumberland temporarily during her third pregnancy, to be near her husband during this anxious time.

The family home, though, was in Filton, Bristol and my mother and I returned there following my birth. During the war years, my mother worked as part of the war effort in Bristol Aircraft Company, which was a prime target for attack. When Mum was away working, my brother and I were looked after by our grandmother.

At the end of the war, my mother was able to continue earning as a seamstress for a men's tailor, making up to ten pairs of trousers each week. I have memories of her sitting at the sewing machine late into the night in order to deliver the completed trousers to the tailor each Friday, when she would also collect the material for new orders.

My father also came from a desperately poor family, being one of fifteen children. He was a bright child and could have had a promising future, had his education continued. However, at 14 years of age he had to leave the school in his small mining village in South Wales, so that he could work in the local coal pit and help support the large family. My dad's father was absent, and my dad helped to support his mother and the surviving nine siblings.

After a number of years working down the pit, and with the closure of coal mines in South Wales, Dad walked to Liverpool where an older sister lived, in order to find work there. It was in Liverpool that he joined the army and spent four years as a young soldier in the King's Regiment in India. He did well, was promoted to the rank of sergeant major, and was offered a commission, but he declined, because he was sending money home to his mother and could not afford to become an officer.

After some years, Dad left the army for civilian life, working in Bristol Aircraft Company as a clerk. He met and married my

mother, but was recalled at the beginning of the Second World
War. He served throughout the war and was demobbed in 1945
with shell shock (now known as post-traumatic stress disorder,
or PTSD). He went straight into hospital in Scotland, where
he remained for more than two years before being transferred
to other hospitals closer to home.

When my father eventually returned home, life changed
again. By this time, I was seven years old and my brother was
four. He and I met Dad for the first time as young children.

Due to my father's shell shock, he was given a modest war
pension and a disability pension. Every couple of years, these
pensions were subject to review, and my dad had to attend
the Department for Work & Pensions in Flower Hill, Bristol,
for an assessment. I remember accompanying my father on
several occasions for this, and I think it was there that I first
observed power and injustice.

I witnessed my father being subjected to harsh questioning
in a bid to reduce his already modest war pension. There was
no doubt in our family that my father's mental health had
suffered due to the Second World War, and these harsh assessments were always dreaded.

When he was able, my father continued to work as a clerk
in the Bristol Aircraft Company. His mental illness was largely
shielded from us children by my mother, but as you can imagine, life was far from smooth, and my brother and I learned
to keep our heads down. Dad's illness continued throughout
the remainder of his lifetime and he had a number of episodes
which resulted in further hospital treatment. This included at
least one attempt on his life.

For many children born during the war years, life was limited, as were our hopes and dreams. It would only be many

years later, as a Christian, that I learned that I could dream of what might be possible.

My mother had the ambition for me to become a secretary and this began at the age of 16. I left school with five O Levels and training in Pitman's shorthand and typewriting. Two weeks after leaving school I started work as a shorthand typist in a large typing pool at W.D. & H.O. Wills, the tobacco manufacturers in Bedminster, Bristol. I started work at 8 a.m. and finished at 6 p.m. for the princely sum of £3 a week. My career as a typist, later to become a secretary, continued through the years in different organizations in Bristol, each time progressing to a better position. My skills as a shorthand typist were to stand me in good stead.

I married at the age of 20 and also at that age learned to drive a car and bought a Capri scooter, which gave me some independence. My marriage was desperately unhappy, though, due to my husband's cruelty and adultery. At that stage, I had a job as secretary to the senior partner in a prestigious architect's practice in Bristol, but I stopped work when I had David, my son, at the age of 25. I suppose I thought things might change, but after having David, life was still terribly unhappy and I came to the realization that I could not continue living in such a poor marriage. My first step was to get a part-time job and then I left my husband, with David aged just 10 months, to start divorce proceedings.

Life as a single, 'supported' parent was difficult. As a divorced woman who was supposed to be receiving maintenance payments for David and myself, I was unable to receive any financial help from the state. In fact, I very rarely received the maintenance payments which had been ordered by the divorce court. So I needed to work in order to support David and myself.

I was suffering from depression and low self-esteem during this time, and looking back, I realize I could easily have fallen into debt and poverty had I not had a skill – typing – to earn money with. Again, as a divorced woman who had been awarded maintenance by a court, I was unable to access free or supported child care from the state. So instead of going out to work, I bought a second-hand manual typewriter and earned money typing at home. In addition, I was fortunate to have a supportive and loving family, something that is not always available to single parents.

I had three jobs, which all involved typing at home. One of these was working for a mail order company, typing envelopes. The reward for typing 1,000 envelopes was just £1. Hard-won remuneration! I also had to collect the envelopes from a city centre office and return them when finished. Another of these jobs involved typing theses for students. The first thesis I undertook was entitled 'Venereal Disease in Bulls' – which was a new area of knowledge for me, and somewhat opened my eyes! However, it also led to me getting part-time employment in the Department of Pathology in the University of Bristol.

Initially, in the Department of Pathology, I worked as a part-time secretary typing postmortem reports. Medical terminology was new to me but I was pleased to extend my skills base. My new salary meant I could afford childcare for David while I worked. The Department of Pathology was also very important to me in that it was here that I met Cliff, who would become my husband.

Cliff was employed as a technician in the department, and he ran the departmental photographic unit. He was required to provide comprehensive film photographic support to a large department, and occasionally needed lots of error-free typing for photography. All of this, of course, was before the age of computing or electric typewriters.

I was not looking for a relationship – let alone marriage – having had such a painful first experience. However, Cliff was altogether different. He was, and remains, so gentle, kind and generous. Cliff got to know more about me through a chance meeting in the Medical School lift one lunchtime. I had been attending car maintenance classes in order to keep my very elderly and needy Mini on the road. Really, all I wanted from the class was how to change the wheels and top up the fluids. They, however, seemed intent on us learning how to take the engine to bits, which was way beyond my capability.

So, back in the lift, I was dressed in a laboratory coat and Cliff asked me what I was doing. I replied that I was going to the car park to take all the wheels off my car. He replied that I couldn't do that. I replied, 'It's my car and I can do what I like.' By the time the lift got to the basement, though, Cliff had convinced me that I should remove just one wheel at a time, especially as the car park was on a slope, which made it generally harder to get the wheels on and off. What's more, he cautioned, if I removed all of them at once, it would be impossible to get any of them back on again. He was right! That conversation broke the ice and we became friends.

Our friendship developed over a year, with David becoming part of the relationship, and I married Cliff in 1971. David was five years old at the time. Our early years together as a family were not without challenges. We lived outside the city and had quite a distance to travel to work, so needed to pay for childcare to collect David from school. Money was always tight. Each month, we had a number of envelopes into which we put money to cover essential outgoings, such as electricity, petrol, oil for the heating and clothing. We always managed – just!

After a couple of years, I needed to increase my hours and it was then that I was asked to become secretary to the Professor of Comparative Pathology. Professor Silver was in fact a veterinary surgeon and his research was with scientists mainly in the US, but also Germany and Hungary as well as the UK. Professor Silver saw me as more than just a secretary, and offered me opportunities to try out new skills. For instance, in his role as consultant veterinary surgeon to Bristol Zoo, he asked me on one occasion to accompany him and provide limited, but crucial, assistance in the artificial insemination of an elephant. I have no idea whether this was successful, but it certainly sticks in my memory!

Professor Silver had a particular interest in injuries sustained by racehorses, as he was involved in developing a way to repair the damaged tendons in their legs using carbon fibre. He would regularly collect amputated horse legs from Newmarket, near where he lived in Cambridge, and bring them with him to work in Bristol. These would arrive in my office in a black dustbin liner, for me to place in deep freeze for later inspection as part of his research for the Horse Race Betting Levy Board.

The work in the Department of Pathology was interesting, but when a job as executive assistant to the university librarian arose, on a higher pay scale, I decided to apply. I was successful, and after twelve years of working in pathology I transferred to the university library. The work was very different indeed, and it was here that I had the opportunity to attend meetings of the University Council and other high-level meetings of governance within the university. I learned how official meetings worked, and observing these gave me an experience of formal processes and proceedings, which would become useful later in life.

I had been a member of the trade union NALGO – the National and Local Government Officers' Association – for most of my time working in the university, but had never held any position until I joined the library. A new opportunity arose within NALGO for a sexual harassment officer and yes, I was persuaded to become that person. This was the 1980s and people were not yet conscious of the importance of tackling sexual harassment at work. Poor Cliff, my husband, still working in the Department of Pathology, had his leg pulled mercilessly when my name was put up around the university as the NALGO sexual harassment officer.

Again, this gave me the opportunity to attend meetings at a high level with management, and the role really opened my eyes to situations that both men and women were subjected to by people in senior positions. On several occasions, I represented female staff members who claimed to have been sexually harassed by men in senior academic positions. I found these situations very difficult, with one side holding far more power than the other. It offended my sense of justice, and I was pleased to be able to stand with the person in the less advantageous position. This was perhaps a precursor of things to come in later life.

Around the age of 40, there was a growing dissatisfaction in me. I began to ask the question, 'Is there more to life than I have yet discovered?' I enjoyed my work, had my wonderful husband and son, but something was niggling. I started visiting different churches over a period of about two years, and eventually found myself going along to the Salvation Army in inner-city Bristol, following an invitation from a friend. I had not realized that the Salvation Army was a church, although I knew about their social work. Bristol Citadel – the Salvation Army's place of worship – was situated in St Paul's, an area of the city that many Bristolians would never go to because of its reputation for crime.

Right from that first visit, I could see that the people there had something I wanted. After four weeks of visiting, I gave my life to Jesus on 25 November 1985, during the Sunday morning service. In his sermon, the preacher invited anyone who did not yet have a relationship with Jesus to come forward. I did not respond by going forward but there, in my seat, quietly in my head, I invited Jesus to come into my life.

Immediately, it felt as though the whole room was filled with light, which poured into me. It was an extraordinary feeling, and so real that I felt sure everyone present could see this river of light pouring down. But it was evident they couldn't – it was just for me. It was God's presence filling me, and it was beautiful.

I really had little idea what I had done, or what it would mean for the remainder of my life, but I knew my life had changed for the good. I told the leaders – called 'Captains' in the Salvation Army – what had happened during the service, and asked if they would meet me to discuss what would come next. They agreed to come to our home the following evening, but encouraged me to tell someone about my experience sooner rather than later.

I returned home to Cliff and David. I clearly remember walking into the house, and saying to Cliff, 'I have something to tell you.' He took one look at me and immediately replied, 'I can see!' God's presence was with me, and I was different.

The following evening, both Cliff and David sat in on my meeting with Captains Chick and Margaret Yuill as they explained to me what it meant to follow Jesus. They were refreshingly straightforward and clearcut in their teaching, and there was no stuffiness. They read and explained the Bible to me, how Jesus had willingly died so we could be free from guilt and shame, and how he had come back to life, showing that God was stronger than evil and death. They explained how life is a battle between good and evil, and that I was now on Jesus' side. It was exactly where I wanted to be!

Cliff and I were warmly welcomed into the fellowship at Bristol Citadel and soon made friends there. We were also both invited to join a homegroup, in which we were welcomed and accepted. Cliff had attended high and moderate Anglican churches as a child and had been a choirboy – in fact, training as a leading soloist up until the age of 14! I had no previous history of church. They really had to start at the beginning with me.

The Army has a strong structure, and various roles within it. I was enrolled as a Salvationist after a year and wore the full uniform – including a bonnet! Cliff chose to join the Salvation Army as an Adherent. An Adherent is the technical term for being a member of the Salvation Army who chooses to follow the rules of the Army but not to take the full vows of a Salvationist. Our spiritual paths were, and remain, strong but different.

Each Sunday, when going into the Citadel for Sunday services, I had to pass men and women lying in the street because of drug and alcohol dependency, and homelessness. This was a new experience for me and one I found difficult, unpleasant even. I was afraid of people who might be out of control or unpredictable, and this was my overriding feeling towards them – fear.

Over the next five or six years, however, God began a change in me towards people on the margins of our society. Slowly, the faces of those I met in the street outside the Citadel began to stay in my mind when I went home, and I prayed for them. I had started to see them not as threats or dangers, but as real, individual people.

I began to speak to these people – to start with, just 'hello,' or 'good morning,' or 'how are you?' Gradually the fear became less. Then one evening, during the sermon, when Captain Yuill was preaching from Isaiah chapter 6, he challenged the congregation with verse 8:

> Then I heard the voice of the Lord saying, 'Whom shall I send? And who will go for us?'

As he read Isaiah's response, 'Here am I. Send me!' I echoed the same words in my heart. There in my seat, in the Citadel that evening, I said to the Lord, 'Here am I. Send me.' And that is the real beginning of my story.

I think from that evening on, I was aware that a big change to my life was about to happen. I was 50 years old – not a classic age to start a big life change, but I had made myself available to God. I didn't even know what I'd made myself available for, though I knew it might not be comfortable! But I was so sure it was right. I had met a God of love, and I wanted to be by his side. He would show me how.

In the meantime, there was more of God's preparation. In 1990, Cliff and I went on a wonderful trip to the Holy Land with a Welsh Baptist minister, the Reverend Albert Turner.

Albert had made it clear to the group that we were not on holiday, rather we were on a pilgrimage – a spiritual journey as well as a geographical one – and this proved to be the case.

The Salvation Army does not practise baptism in water, but does not ban Salvationists from being baptized in another church if they wish to be. As a Baptist, Albert was, naturally, unimpressed that I had not been baptized and so, on my two-week trip, I had evening lessons from him about baptism. This resulted in me being baptized by total immersion in the Sea of Galilee!

As I came up from the water, I knew the presence of the Holy Spirit. There was a tangible warmth in my heart. I felt amazing release from past hurt and shame, a sense of guilt being washed right away. Cliff could see it too – I was lighter and more joyous.

The two weeks Cliff and I spent together in Israel were illuminating, as we walked on ground that Jesus would have walked upon, and had the Bible opened up to us by Albert. Albert read the relevant passages at every place we visited.

We stayed in Palestinian hotels and were treated as special guests. Because of Albert's connections with the Palestinian people over more than twenty years, we were invited into the home of a Muslim family during Ramadan. Six of us from the group went in taxis to Bethany and were served a delicious traditional Palestinian meal by the family. They were so welcoming, and delighted to invite us into their home. Because the sun had not yet set, they did not join us in eating the meal. Nonetheless, the whole experience was of sharing life, love, food and a generosity of spirit across our differences.

One day, during our time in Jerusalem, after I'd been baptized, we needed to find a bank, and it was here that I discovered

I could understand Hebrew! As I walked in, I realized that the leaflets and notices in the bank were all clear to me in what they said. Everywhere around me – in posters, signs, even in a newspaper – I could read the Hebrew language fluently. It was extraordinary. I had previously not had training in any foreign language, let alone Hebrew. I can't explain it, and I don't know how it happened, except that it must have been the Holy Spirit. It proved to be a useful spiritual gift during our pilgrimage, but sadly, I found that I no longer had the gift when we returned home.

On the final day of our 'holiday' we visited St George's Cathedral in Jerusalem. Unusually, there were no other visitors in the church, and we went into the side chapel to pray together. I have to admit to being a bit impatient to go and spend my last few shekels, but somewhat reluctantly Cliff and I chose a place to sit.

At my feet was a hassock which was slightly in the way, so I bent down to move it. To my astonishment, I saw that it was embroidered on one side with the emblem of the Salvation Army, which is quite distinctive. When I turned it over, I was even more astonished to see that it had come from Newbiggin-by-the-Sea, Northumberland – the very small town where I had been born in 1941!

Of all the places we could have chosen to sit, I had been led to that one. I knew that this was no coincidence. It was confirmation that I, from my small beginnings, who had met God through the Salvation Army, was in the right place at the right time as far as God was concerned.

God was on my case. I'd offered my availability, and he was taking me up on it! My heart swelled with wonder, but also with a degree of trepidation.

3

Lighting the Candle

It was several months after my time in Israel that the next step in my journey took place. Captains Chick and Margaret Yuill had moved on from Bristol and had been replaced by Captains Melvyn and Cath Jones. They, and the leadership team in Bristol, agreed that an office worker was needed to deal with the daily administration of the Citadel, and I was asked if I would be interested.

I thanked them, but politely said no. I did, though, say that I would be interested in working in the community surrounding the Citadel! This is where God had brought me – from being afraid of the people on the streets of St Paul's, to actually wanting to love and serve them in some way.

The Captains had not been expecting this response at all, but they took it seriously. They decided the idea needed praying about, and the Citadel's Corps (those actively interested in serving the local community) held a day of prayer together. This resulted in me being tasked to work as a full-time community worker.

I was actually given the title of community manager, which I remember felt somewhat unrealistic. There was nothing and no one to manage, and I had no experience of working in a community, having spent my entire working career as a secretary in an office, following someone else's lead.

Yet, despite the uncertainty, Cliff and I were confident that God was leading us. Believing this, I resigned from my job at Bristol University Library, despite having worked for the university for the past twenty-five years. This was very scary for us as a family, because I was the main breadwinner, and the salary on offer in the Salvation Army was less than half what I had been earning. But at the beginning of August 1991, I turned up for work as the community manager of the Salvation Army's Candle Project.

The project was named after the proverb 'It is better to light a small candle than to curse the darkness'. Well, I felt like a very small candle indeed! My office was a semi-converted broom cupboard in a semi-derelict hall alongside the Citadel on Ashley Road, St Paul's, inner-city Bristol. I felt inadequate, unprepared and had no idea where this was going to lead. I was terrified. Yet, I was confident that it was God's calling. My prayer then, and over the following years, was that God would equip me for the work he had called me to do, as I was only too aware that in my own strength, I would fail, miserably.

It was a drastic shock to the system. I went from working as a member of a large team of people in the University Library, where my office had been comfortable, warm and safe, to operating alone in a semi-converted cupboard with only the brooms for company.

Cliff set me up with an elderly IBM golf ball electric typewriter, which had been discarded from the university because they had moved into computing, and that was all the equipment I had. Not even a telephone. The Candle Project received no official funding from the Salvation Army and would have to depend on its charity shop, Magpie, and my fundraising efforts through speaking in churches and small groups, to provide money and donated food items.

How do you start a community project when you are working alone, know very little about the needs of the people you hope to reach and, perhaps more importantly, are not streetwise in an area like inner-city St Paul's? I was 50 years of age, with some life experience, and very aware of God's leading. I used what I had – a bit of common sense and some imperfectly honed gumption.

I decided that I needed to walk the streets of St Paul's each morning, getting to know the local people – the shopkeepers, the homeless people and even the drug dealers. I needed to be known, and to know who I was dealing with.

This was not as difficult as it first appeared, because as soon as the homeless, and people in need, were aware that someone was available in the building each weekday, they started to come to me. Initially I just made copious cups of tea and coffee with biscuits. In the autumn of 1991, I added toast! All this took place in the Salvation Army building, which was not in a great state of repair.

It was not long before I was asked for blankets and warm bedding and so, in my naïve enthusiasm, I rang friends and gathered together a number of sleeping bags.

Word quickly spread that sleeping bags were available at the Bristol Citadel and, on that first morning, together with tea and coffee, bags were handed out to homeless men. And here is where I made my first mistake. I had yet to establish a dependable supply of sleeping bags, but I had created an expectation. A homeless man, Steve, whom I had seen behaving very badly on the streets due to alcohol dependency, came into the hall. Steve was very drunk and demanded a sleeping bag. I politely apologized and said that I had given out all the ones I had, but would try to get one for him the following day. That, of course, would not do for him and he started pushing me around the room, demanding a sleeping bag.

I was terrified. But, to my surprise and everlasting gratitude, another of the alcoholic men, a very large Irish man, got up and came to my rescue. He picked Steve up by the scruff of his neck and shouted, 'The lady said she hasn't got any more sleeping bags! Got it?' He then dropped Steve back down again on the floor. Steve scuttled off and I learned a hard lesson – never promise anything you cannot deliver.

However, I had learned something else – to have been defended like this, I must have earned a small place of trust in that community of homeless men. I was immensely grateful to God, and also to Seamus, the large Irish man.

Seamus, like the majority of men coming for a cup of tea, was homeless and alcoholic. Their preferred drink was a cheap and very strong cider, but when times were hard, they would drink methylated spirits. This was even cheaper, but has devastating and lasting effects, such as convulsions, respiratory problems and even blindness.

I was returning to Candle one afternoon after posting some letters, when I saw a man writhing around on the pavement. I crossed over the road and saw that it was Seamus. He was screaming in terror and lashing out with his arms. He was fitting, and it was apparent that he could see animals attacking him and was clearly terrified. I had never before seen *delirium tremens* but that's what it was – one of the shocking effects of long-term alcohol addiction. I tried to speak to him but quickly realized that Seamus needed medical help and asked the local shopkeeper to call an ambulance. Seamus died within months of this encounter, and I was hugely saddened at losing a friend.

Over the first six months or so of walking the streets, I gradually got to know people and places 'of interest'. One of these places was an infamous café, the Black and White Café, on Grosvenor Road, St Paul's. The Black and White was a crucial community hub. For many years, it was the main drug distribution centre for the whole of the West Country, and I was informed by Avon and Somerset Police that 2 per cent of the entire nation's crime took place on Grosvenor Road at that time. I decided that I needed to make myself known in the Black and White.

Feeling not at all brave, I marched in. Loud music was playing, and the place was in darkness – I could barely see anybody or anything. I raised my voice tentatively over the music and started off by saying, 'Hello, I have come to introduce myself.' Immediately, the music stopped and from within the darkness a male voice said, 'We know who you are, lady!'

I will never know who was there, but I had evidently made a mark! They made clear that I wasn't welcome in the café, but that didn't matter – I had overcome my fear and faced them on their territory. I left, carrying with me the strong aroma of cannabis, and continued my walk, relieved that another hurdle had been cleared.

During those first months, I prayed as much as I worked for the Candle Project. I prayed alone at home, I prayed with Cliff, and I prayed with other members of the Citadel. I was acutely aware of how much I needed God's presence with me. The work at the Candle Project quickly grew and God answered prayer in many ways – through volunteers, through resources and gifts, and by changing people's lives.

In the month of December 1991, just sixteen weeks since the Candle Project started, we served 206 cooked meals from the Citadel, including hosting almost 100 people for a Christmas dinner. We gave out eighty-eight emergency food parcels, eighty-one sleeping bags and forty-eight Christmas hampers, many of them including toys for children. Within twelve months of opening, I had two volunteers helping me, and we had around sixty people a day coming in for hot drinks and a snack.

I quickly learned that you can't assume anything about needy people. The men and women who came into the Candle Project drop-in were from backgrounds which were sometimes surprising. For instance, there was a handsome alcoholic man whose family were aristocracy. He was a very troubled young man, who I was told was abusive to women, although he was always polite when I saw him in the drop-in. Both this young man, and another young man, requested that we provide *The Guardian* and *The Times* newspapers each day and they avidly read these while enjoying coffee and a snack. They also enjoyed a game of chess when they were both sober enough to do so – but this was not often. Both were homeless and had chaotic lifestyles.

The second young man who loved to read the newspapers was called Marcus. He was alcoholic. He came from Wales, he told me, and had attended university, although had dropped out before completing his course. Over the years that I knew Marcus, he spoke about a young daughter in Wales and at Christmas, birthdays and Easter, he would ask for gifts to send on to his daughter. On one occasion, he asked us for the train fare to go to his father's funeral in Cardiff.

Marcus was charming, articulate, but wayward and badly behaved. His life began to spiral out of control. Eventually he asked for help, saying he wanted to change. I made enquiries on his behalf and it was decided that he would go to Pilsdon Community in Dorset in order to recover. Pilsdon is an inclusive, welcoming, restorative community run on Christian principles, and has a history of supporting hundreds of people over the years, in their times of need. Guests are expected to work on the farm or in the garden, in order to contribute to the community. Many people find healing, wholeness and a spiritual awakening there.

Marcus was driven to Pilsdon and left in the care of the Reverend Peter Barnett, who had once been the parish priest in St Agnes Church, St Paul's, but was now the community's warden. We heard nothing more from him for about ten or eleven months until one day, who should walk into the drop-in but Marcus. He looked well – healthy and happy. He had put on some weight, and had a smile on his face that warmed my heart. Marcus announced that he was sober, and that he was now a shepherd. He was rightly very proud of both these things. As you can well imagine, this transformation caused quite a stir in the drop-in with those who had known Marcus in his former life.

It was a wonderful, encouraging gift to me to see Marcus looking healthy and seemingly motivated towards a more fulfilling life. However, I was anxiously aware that he had decided to return to Bristol with nowhere to live and no plans for the future. Sadly, perhaps inevitably, he deteriorated and once again lost control of his life due to his drinking. Tragically, Marcus died when he was still in his early thirties.

Sister Annaliese, an Anglican nun living and working in St Paul's, had also on many occasions helped Marcus, and was becoming a trusted friend of mine. With heavy hearts, we drove together to Wiltshire to attend this funeral of a man we thought we had known quite well. Soon after arriving, though, we were astonished to discover that Marcus was not his name at all, that he did not have a daughter in Wales, and that his father, whom we had thought dead, was sitting in the front row next to his mum!

Sister Annaliese and I drove back to Bristol together following the funeral, awash with contrasting emotions. We laughed and cried in equal measure. We had both loved him for who he was, regardless of his name, family or circumstances, and we were both heartbroken.

Knowing Marcus gave me another understanding of the reality of life on the streets. This young, homeless man, who really had nothing, had lived on the dream of a relationship and a beautiful young daughter. Marcus got under my skin. I'd always seen the potential in him. I remember my heart being so warmed when he came and announced so proudly that he was a shepherd, and I remember the despair in me as I watched him get sucked back into a life of alcoholism and demise. We prayed for him, we loved him, but we still lost him.

Through the Candle Project, I got to know a number of ex-servicemen who found life on civvy street impossible to negotiate. One of these men – Sam – became a trusted and valuable volunteer, and eventually a paid cleaner for the project. Sadly, though, his addictions eventually got the better of him and he died of an overdose. Again, it was not difficult to see the potential in this man. He was a gifted artist and generous with his time. I could rely on Sam whenever I needed help. He kept a low profile and worked quietly in the background to make sure that things worked as best they could in the drop-in. Sam touched the lives of all who knew him, and

Cliff and I were deeply saddened by his death. He had become a true friend.

Within two years of the Candle Project starting, our regulars had grown to around one hundred and twenty people a day, six days a week. Our volunteer numbers had also increased – and without them, the work could not have continued. We cooked a two-course meal every single Sunday for around a hundred people. This often included ever-more imaginative ways of incorporating corned beef, huge quantities of which had been donated to the Salvation Army from the EU beef mountain!

Although it was wonderful to see our visitors eagerly consuming these meals, we could never just sit back and enjoy seeing them be well-fed and looked after. They were often disorderly due to alcohol and drug use, and fights sometimes broke out in the somewhat crowded conditions. We were always on the alert!

Two things were becoming clear. Firstly, that we had outgrown the facilities that the old building could provide, and secondly, that someone was needed to work alongside me, to share the responsibilities.

A woman from Bristol Citadel fellowship, Marilyn Paine, was appointed to work alongside me. Marilyn had a heart for the marginalized and came from a long line of Salvationists, her parents having been officers. Marilyn and I worked well together, and it was wonderful to share the load with a like-minded person. Marilyn was a gift to the project and to me. We rely on God, but we also need other human beings to lean on and work his purposes with.

The men and women we worked with had complex, multiple needs. These included alcoholism, drug dependency, family breakdown, material poverty, relationship breakdown, mental

health issues, physical disabilities and illnesses, violence, un-
employment and low levels of education or qualification. This
was in addition to their emotional and spiritual need for security, care and a God who accepted, loved and could overcome
for them. Working with such people – finding a way through
all their problems – is not straightforward.

One of these people was a very special man, who had been
my first friend when I started working in the Candle Project in
1991. His name was Tom. He was alcoholic and a dwarf. He
was also extremely streetwise. Tom befriended me and helped
me through times of naïvety, gullibility and inexperience. He
gently 'educated' me about surviving in St Paul's, tipping me
off about people and places to avoid, and who fitted in where
in the community's hierarchies.

I used to run informal Bible studies on some of the afternoons, and it was during one of these that I asked a small
group of men if there was something they would like to look
at or discuss from the Bible. Tom – a regular attender of my
studies – immediately said he liked the story of David and
Goliath and so we read 1 Samuel 17 together. Then, to everyone's surprise, Tom attempted, with some help, to climb onto
a chair. He was quite inebriated, but he stood up on that chair,
raised his arm as though holding a slingshot, and declared that
he knew what the Goliath in his life was – it was the booze.
We were all very moved and the four other men in the group
all agreed that this was also the truth for them.

Accepting that you have a problem is the first step towards
solving it, but it's no guarantee. Tom's life, like those of the
other men, was a messy web of problems and challenges. After being homeless for several years, he was at last allocated a
basement flat in St Paul's, which initially was very helpful to

him. However, it was quickly taken over by other homeless, heavy-drinking men who were bigger and stronger than Tom, and the place was soon wrecked.

Tom approached me at this point, and asked me to help clean it up. With the help of two willing friends, I gathered cleaning materials and buckets and went over to his flat. As we walked through the front door of the basement flat, I saw that Tom was helping himself to free electricity! Six-inch nails had been hammered into the electricity supply cable to the upstairs flat, and using car jump-start leads, Tom had made a connection to supply his own flat!

I may have been briefly appalled by this lack of moral judgement, but such thoughts were quickly overshadowed as we waded into the absolute filth of Tom's flat. We were assailed by the smell of human waste. Broken glass was scattered over the floor, alongside litter and debris, and the windows, walls and floors had excrement spread over them. The whole place was revolting. Tom's bed was also covered in excrement and pee, and all of his bedding had to be bundled into bin liners.

It took three of us the entire day to clean that tiny flat. We had to have the glass in a window replaced to make the flat safe again. Later in the day, I made a visit to the Salvation Army charity shop, Magpie, which was also known as 'The 50p Shop', and collected clean bedding, crockery and cutlery. It was hard work, but the flat looked and smelt a whole lot better by the time we had finished.

Tom's flat was quite a revelation to me of how bad things could get. It's easy to think that the answer to homelessness is to find someone a home, and the city council were able to do this for Tom, but there was so much more than that to solving the problems in his life.

At the end of that day, I well remember longing to get home and have a good, hot shower. That was the first time I practised letting the filth go down the plughole and not letting it slime me up. I was part of Tom's life, but if I allowed myself to be dragged down by the sadness, the despair, the filth, I would not be able to help him any more. I couldn't help but be affected, but I needed to be able to step away as well, back into my place of safety and wholeness. This is something I was only beginning to understand.

It was not long after that occasion, one morning in the late spring of 1993, that a young homeless woman banged on the door of the drop-in while I was getting ready to open. She said that Tom was lying on the street about 100 yards down Ashley Road, and that he was ill. I immediately left my office and ran down the road and there was Tom, propped up against a shop window. He was clearly very poorly, in pain and not breathing well. I told him I would go back to my office to ring for an ambulance. 'It's too late,' he mumbled, but I ran off anyway. I looked back at Tom as I ran, and he flopped a limp hand against his mouth, to blow me a kiss. By the time I returned to him about ten minutes later, I saw that he had died.

I was distraught. Tom had been my first friend in the homeless community, offering me unconditional friendship. In those early days of Candle, it was this lovely man who had looked out for me, taking on a role as my defender and mentor. He had realized my vulnerability perhaps even more than I did. I had seen him try to face his problems, been there for his ups and his downs. I had seen him meet God. I'd seen him show love to other people, and I'd been a recipient of that love, but I hadn't been able to rescue him.

The Salvation Army held a funeral for Tom which was absolutely packed with his friends. Tom's favourite piece of music was 'Lord of the Dance' and the Salvation Army band played this beautifully. It was so bittersweet – a lively, joyful, hope-filled song for this life so tragically cut short. It was a very emotional time for us all.

Tom's mother had lost contact with him some years before I met him, but the Salvation Army have a service for finding people, and they were able to track her down. She lived in Bristol, and was informed of Tom's death. She did not feel able to come to the funeral, but afterwards, I asked her if I could visit, and she welcomed this. It was really good to be able to share with her some of the brighter moments of Tom's life, and how loved he had been by everyone at Candle and at Bristol Citadel. I took her the only possession Tom had left when he died. It was a Salvation Army song book.

As is so often the case, there are humorous memories for me alongside the grief and sadness of Tom's funeral. About two dozen of Tom's friends had said they wanted to attend both the funeral service and the cremation which followed it. All of them were from the homeless community and in varying states of sobriety. One particular man, though, who was well known for his violent behaviour when drunk, began to get out of control during the funeral service.

I was concerned that if he continued in that manner, and also continued drinking, he would disrupt the service in the crematorium. I therefore briefly slipped out of the funeral and rang the St Paul's police team, who were already on the alert because of this gathering. I told them who it was, they agreed to help out, and we left it at that.

At the end of the funeral service, we organized lifts for Tom's friends to the crematorium, which was about three miles away. I was busy helping people get into the right vehicles and set off in the right direction, so I didn't notice the unmarked police car pick up our troublesome friend. I learned the following day from him that he had got into a car, thinking he was getting a lift to the crem, and was in fact taken about ten miles out of the city and left to walk back to St Paul's. He was very grumpy – and I have to admit that I did not let on that I had anything to do with it!

By the summer of 1993, just two years into the Candle Project, Tom's was the seventh tragic and untimely death among the homeless community we were serving. With each loss, my heart was breaking into more and more pieces. And yet, the project was a success – we were giving out so much of God's love in practical, meaningful ways to those who needed it. That summer alone, we cooked 796 Sunday lunches, gave out 1,344 emergency food parcels, helped 137 people with clothing and household items, and delivered 100 counselling sessions – for alcohol/drug abuse, homelessness, violence, prostitution, bereavement, depression and other needs.

We had also started giving people advice and help with form-filling, housing and debt. And because in 1993 it was still possible for a householder's water supply to be disconnected due to non-payment of bills, we helped manage bill payments, and get electricity and water supplies reconnected.

We were also meeting a spiritual need – we were showing people a God of love, acceptance and kindness, and many responded.

All this from me saying to God, 'I'm available. Use me.' But I did start to wonder, for how long could I keep being used, before being all used up?

4

Building and Belonging

Our work was being blessed, and growing. With all this activity, it became clear that the needs of the people – and our growing ability to meet those needs – were more than the existing semi-derelict building with its limited facilities could manage. The roof was leaking badly, the equipment was outdated, and the furnishings were really beyond repair. We needed a major refurb.

The Citadel fellowship started a building fund. It would need a huge amount of money, but within a short space of time, amazingly, we were to raise more than £250,000 to refurbish our hall – £150,000 of this total came in two extraordinary bequests.

A lady in our congregation worked in the Bristol & West building society, and took some of the building fund leaflets to put in the public area. An elderly man came into the building society and picked one up. He asked the lady if she knew anything about this project and she told him she was a part of the fellowship, and explained as much as she could about the work. That was all the contact we ever had with the man, but he died two weeks later and left £75,000 to the Candle Project building fund.

Just a fortnight after this, a second bequest came to us via the Salvation Army's national headquarters. Another elderly man, in another part of the country, had specified in his will that he wanted to support the work of an inner-city Salvation Army fellowship working with the homeless. It seems that the Candle Project was the only one at that time which fulfilled those criteria, and so we received a second sum of £75,000.

I was absolutely blown away by this miraculous provision. It was so amazing to see God at work in response to our prayers, and with the money came a renewed sense of purpose and energy. Planning for the new centre began.

In order to raise the remaining funds needed for the refurbishment, I went on a speaking tour to many different churches and agencies in Bristol and the surrounding areas. This was quite an undertaking and well outside my comfort zone (I can't remember when I'd last been inside my comfort zone, mind you!). I had to speak to large groups of people in churches and in halls, something I'd never done before. This was in addition to my six-days-a-week work in the drop-in.

It was terrifying and tiring, standing up in front of people that I didn't know, in my Salvation Army uniform, sometimes holding a lit candle, and trying to explain about my work, then asking for money. However, people were moved and responded generously. Bit by bit, the remaining £100,000 came in – enough to undertake the necessary building work.

In addition, as more people came to learn about our project, we attracted resources in the form of volunteer helpers from a range of churches across the city. Among these was a man who would become a good friend to me personally, and also to David, my son. John Stradling was his name. John was a retired farmer, carpenter and a truly remarkable and lovely human being who had a heart for the homeless. In particular, John's heart was in equipping men with skills for possible employment. He was also active in helping them at times of rehousing, particularly when they were able to move into unfurnished accommodation. This is always a difficult move – people are given four walls, but have nothing in the way of furniture and fittings to put in it.

John collected furniture which was unwanted and often in a poor state of repair. He then worked alongside the men being rehoused, using a workshop he rented locally, to repair and restore the pieces. The outcome was quite remarkable – not only were there now useable tables, chairs and sofas to furnish the men's houses, but they themselves had learned new and useful skills. They had a great sense of purpose in creating and repairing furniture for their own homes. Anything that was not needed for people being rehoused was sold, and the money used to purchase tools and equipment. John was a visionary and became very well known in his blue transit-type van, buzzing around St Paul's.

It became clear that renovating the old Salvation Army centre would take time, and that we would have to vacate the building while it was done. How could we do this and continue to serve the community who came to us daily for help? We realized we had to find alternative, local accommodation for our rather unusual needs.

We made enquiries in the surrounding area, and it was John Stradling who identified an unused shop on Ashley Road, about 100 yards from our building. It was called 'M&N Electrical'. This was, in fact, the same shop that Tom had died outside earlier that year. John discovered that the owner of the shop was a Muslim man and he approached him to ask if we could view the building, making it clear what we intended and the fact that we had no money for rent! The owner agreed to a viewing, and gave us a key.

John and I went to the M&N Electrical shop on Ashley Road and opened the door. It was a bit of a shock, to say the least. Not only were there no furniture or fittings, but there were very few floorboards – and those that were there were rotten. It was one single, large room, no plaster on the walls and only one window – bricked up. I was horrified – it didn't look like it could be of any use to us at all.

John, however, looked at it through different eyes, and was inspired. 'It's perfect!' he declared. I remember thinking, 'Perfect for what?' However, I believed in him and together we got permission from Captain Jones, my boss, to go ahead with restoration work to make M&N Electrical temporarily habitable. There was one condition – no money was available whatsoever: all the building fund money had to go into refurbishing the main building.

The following day, during the morning drop-in, John and I announced to a bewildered group of people that we needed to close our building for a few months and move the drop-in to M&N Electrical. We explained that before this could happen, essential work was needed in our temporary premises. We had to install a sink unit, obtain a cooker, carry out electrical work, and – oh yes – put a floor in! And there was no money to buy anything.

The response was truly wonderful. One by one, voices were raised from around the drop-in: 'I'm a sparky – I'll lend a hand!' 'I'm a plumber – I can get the sink in.' 'I'm a chippy, me, I can help out!' And so we had a workforce . . . but as yet, no materials.

However, word got round quickly. That same day, men started appearing outside the shop bearing 'gifts'. One brought some floorboards, another had a previously loved sink unit. Yet another turned up with an elderly electric cooker in tow. I decided not to ask necessarily where all these 'gifts' came from – it was provision and we accepted it gratefully. So, work began, with John supervising the refurbishment. It was incredibly uplifting to see those men working with pride and a sense of ownership on our new temporary drop-in premises.

We were able to move into M&N Electrical before the onset of winter 1993. Because the room was a fraction of the size of our main building, we had to monitor numbers coming in at any one time, and manage things differently. There was no storage capacity of any kind, so we had to carry food and supplies to and fro every day. But it worked. We were even able to provide a hot Sunday lunch for anyone who wanted it – though it was admittedly only one course!

Amazingly, during the ten months or so we were in M&N Electrical, and despite the somewhat cramped accommodation, we did not have a single fight. I put that down to the pride and sense of ownership the men had. They themselves had equipped and provided the space they were now using. Those months were hard work, but it was actually a very happy time for our drop-in community.

Help also sometimes came from unexpected sources, and this was the case when the Bridgwater Chapter of the Harley Owners Group contacted me and said they would like to support our work. Sure enough, one Saturday afternoon in March 1994, a group of thirty or so gleaming Harley-Davidson motorcycles and their riders arrived at Bristol Citadel bearing gifts of food, blankets and clothing for the homeless. After we had shared tea and cakes with them, I was given an offer too good to turn down – to ride pillion around St Paul's. It did wonders for my street cred! It was also great fun. To top it all, a photograph of me on the Harley made the centre page of *The War Cry*, the Salvation Army national newspaper!

All those gleaming motorbikes parked neatly outside Bristol Citadel was a sight I shall never forget – and neither will the residents of St Paul's. When the time came for us to move into the refurbished building, John went to see the owner of M&N again to ask about rent. This generous-hearted Muslim man refused payment of any kind and said he had been pleased to help. He was of course also happy for us to leave the sink unit and the old cooker, together with the flooring, so we felt we had made some contribution! Without his kindness, and without John's practical help during this period in the Candle Project, we should have been forced to close the drop-in throughout the cold winter months. I could never have coordinated the practical work like he did. John was a wonderful gift to us all and a very dear friend to me.

In summer 1994, the time came for us to move back into the refurbished building. Careful planning had taken place to provide for the needs of the homeless community. We now had a fully equipped kitchen to enable us to cater for large numbers of people, together with a shower and a bath, with a hoist to help those with mobility issues. We also had heavy-duty washing machines to enable clothing to be cleaned. This was quite a step up in what we could offer. The Salvation Army charity shop, Magpie, provided clean clothing at a cost of 50p per item (20p for children's clothing) when needed. Most importantly, we had a medical room.

Over many months in 1992–93 I had written to the health secretary, William Waldegrave, expressing my concerns over the lack of healthcare for homeless people. It was a catch-22 situation – if they had no fixed abode, they were unable to register in a GP practice, and without a GP they fell through the safety net of the healthcare system.

Also, the simple practice that most of us take for granted – that we make an appointment, and go to the doctor when the day and time for that appointment comes – is actually out of reach for a homeless person with a chaotic life. Who knows how sober they will be when that time comes? How will they get to the doctors' surgery? How can they have the presence and wherewithal to attend a medical appointment when they don't really know where they will sleep tonight, or what they will eat for their next meal? It's unrealistic.

William Waldegrave eventually visited Bristol (not the Candle Project) and put into place the HASH system, which stood for Healthcare and Advice for the Single Homeless. This was a clinic based in a hostel for the homeless in Jamaica Street, St Paul's. We managed to get agreement that the HASH team doctor and nurse would come to the refurbished Candle Project once a week on a Tuesday morning to treat minor injuries and health needs on-site. This was an important step forward in bringing provision within reach of those who needed it. It was well used, with a good number of people seeking advice or treatment in the well-known surroundings of Candle for medical issues they would probably not have gone to a surgery or clinic for.

The medical room was small, with two chairs, a desk and some shelves with basic equipment. It was accessed through a door off the main drop-in room, so it was also private, which was vital. I was proud of it.

It was a wonderful feeling to move into that newly rebuilt and repurposed building. There was a real joy in the cleanness and newness of the place, which reflected in the self-esteem of the men and women who came into the drop-in. The very fabric of the building was more evidence that they were cared for, cared about. And, of course, we could meet their needs like we hadn't before.

The everyday work in the drop-in continued, and continued growing. No day was without its successes, often in small ways – someone being able to have a shower and get themselves and their clothes clean, for example, or get medical advice where they wouldn't have before. We also had drug and alcohol services coming in on a weekly basis to talk to people and advise them.

A good number of men took advantage of these services, which could lead to taking more control of their lives. Because of the space and environment, we were able to engage with drop-in users in a completely different way. This gave opportunities to discuss housing needs, and to signpost to other services, and importantly, once people have their immediate physical needs met, they are freer to receive emotionally and spiritually.

The Easter after we moved into the new building, invitations were given out to the services which took place each evening during Holy Week. On Maundy Thursday, a small group of men from the drop-in came along when the Captain was washing the feet of the attendees. I found it precious to see them witnessing a leader modelling Jesus' humility in serving others. We had a life-size cross in the Citadel, and the chairs were arranged around it. Later in the service, every one of those men went forward and knelt at the cross.

5

Flopping Sideways

In the years I ran the Candle Project, it was possible to get men into treatment centres for their addictions if they had reached the point of wanting to change. One such treatment centre, which was run by the Salvation Army, was in Southampton – the Mountbatten Centre. I drove several of our clients to Southampton when they expressed a desire to change, and when I thought they might be ready for treatment. Those journeys were quite emotional for the men, and not particularly easy for me. The men were often very drunk and I learned not to allow them to sit alongside me in the front of the car because they kept flopping sideways onto me as I was driving.

On another occasion, before taking someone to Southampton for treatment I had to take his beloved dog to a kennel for safekeeping. Unfortunately for the dog and for the car, the dog was completely loused up and I had to announce to my poor husband that we needed to disinfect the car. Cliff was, as always, so understanding and took on the job of cleaning our car.

On one occasion, I took a man called Oliver to the Mountbatten Centre. He was apprehensive but knew that change was needed. Having left him there, I started my drive back to Bristol but stopped off to have something to eat, and got back to Bristol fairly late that night. In the morning, when I arrived as usual at the Candle Project, there was Oliver, the man I had taken to Southampton the previous afternoon. It seems that he changed his mind about treatment and managed to thumb a lift back to Bristol, probably arriving back in the city before me. Not his time for change, sadly. He died shortly after.

On reflection, I realized that perhaps I wanted these men to go into treatment when they were not totally committed to change at that time. Change is so difficult for anyone suffering from an addiction and only that person can make the decision and see it through. No well-meaning person can make the decision for them.

Sometimes an addict might feel genuinely ready to change, but you still don't know for sure whether it will work. You do your best to decide whether it's a good time to offer the chance – there's never a guarantee. Sometimes I think about Jesus dying on the cross, not knowing, when he made that decision, whether we would accept his loving sacrifice or not. He did it for the chance that he might save us.

Work in the project continued, with ever-more people coming to the centre for help or just something to eat. We constantly saw improvements, but sadly, the number of deaths went on increasing. Men I had known and grown to love were dying because of drug and alcohol abuse and homelessness. I began to feel overwhelmed with sadness and grief, together with a sense of real physical exhaustion. I was also having difficulty in praying. Where was God in all this suffering?

One Wednesday afternoon when the drop-in had closed and all the volunteers had left the building, I was alone tidying up. I heard footsteps and saw a fairly new drop-in user crossing the floor towards me. I was surprised because I had thought the door had been closed and locked – it seemed it had not. To have this particular man in an otherwise empty building was immediately worrying as he had not long left Broadmoor, a high-security psychiatric hospital, having committed murder. He was also a heavy drinker.

This man, Stanley, just kept walking towards me, right up to me, and then started pushing me against a wall. He pulled out a knife and held it against my throat, never taking his eyes off my face, not saying a word. I was completely immobilized and unable to respond in any way. I didn't pray or speak or try to get away. It was like I was paralysed. My heart pounded.

And then something extraordinary happened. My son, David, unusually, had been passing the Candle Project and saw that the door was open. He walked in, saw what was happening, and immediately ran towards me and Stanley, shouting as he did so.

As David came towards us, something clicked back on inside me, and my reactions returned. But instead of trying to get away from Stanley, my mothering instincts kicked in, and I tried to protect David from him instead, pushing David away so that Stanley wouldn't stab him. It sounds crazy, perhaps, but my only thoughts were that I didn't want my son harmed, and that fired me into action.

David, though, is more than 6ft tall, strong and well-built. Stanley was average height but painfully thin. David took hold of Stanley and pushed him away, taking control of the situation, making sure that Stanley was not within striking distance of either of us. Before we really knew what was happening, Stanley then slashed his own face and quietly walked away and out of the building.

No words had been exchanged between Stanley, David and me. It all happened quickly and ended without a word being spoken. But I have no doubt that David saved me from serious injury, or worse, that day, and I have no doubt that God saved me by bringing David along at exactly the right moment.

God also saved me from my own foolishness, at being alone and vulnerable in the building, without having checked the front door. I made many mistakes in those early days. In fact, I made many mistakes in later days, too, but I believe God saw my heart, and he honoured me for that. I think God is more interested in us being willing to do something than in us always doing it right.

There were very few knife incidents over the time I worked at the Candle Project, but fear and violence did always tremor beneath the surface of our work.

There was another man, who we had spent a lot of time with, helping him to access housing, and to take steps to address his alcohol and drug problem. He was making significant progress, and I can only think that he was attempting to thank us when, one afternoon, he sidled up to me conspiratorially and offered me the use of 'a shooter' in case I wanted to get rid of my 'old man'.

He said that I could have the gun for £20 for the weekend, but would have to pay extra if I used it! I thanked him but explained that I loved Cliff, that I on no account wanted to get rid of him, and that I wouldn't be taking him up on his kind offer!

It was on another Wednesday afternoon around one o'clock when I was returning from the local bakery, that a car screeched to a halt alongside me on Ashley Road. The passenger door of the car opened and a large bundle was pushed out, into the street. I looked around to see if anyone else was there to investigate this bundle – there was no one. As I approached, I could see that the bundle was in fact a woman, and I recognized her. She was a sex worker who often stood on the pavement outside my office, working.

Although I had tried for many months to engage with this woman, Ann, she would have nothing to do with me, and just gave me lots of verbal abuse – telling me where to go and calling me names. She was still not at all impressed to see me that afternoon, as she lay crumpled and bundled up in the road, but she agreed to let me help. Ann had been raped and stabbed. I could see the stab wound in her belly. I helped her into my office and she agreed that I could take her to Accident & Emergency in the Bristol Royal Infirmary. She was quickly taken in to be seen, while I waited for her. After a few minutes, a doctor came out, and invited me into her cubicle saying that Ann had something to tell me.

Without any emotion, Ann told me that she was pregnant, that a bed had been secured for her in the local maternity hospital, and that I needed to take her there – immediately. She had not been aware of her pregnancy, which is not unusual in drug users. Often, they are malnourished, and their body weight is so low that they no longer menstruate reliably, and therefore can't tell when their cycle changes. Ann continued verbally abusing me, even as I drove her the short journey to the maternity hospital and left her in the care of the medical staff.

The following morning, I received a telephone call from Ann, saying that she had given birth to a daughter, and announcing aggressively that now was the time for me to provide the help that I'd so often offered. In short, she needed everything for a baby.

I rang a local church who had already been generous to the project, and asked for their help. Within a week, they gathered together a Moses basket, bedding, clothing, nappies and everything required to look after a new-born. Ann and her daughter left hospital and moved in with one of her friends, in a basement squat on Ashley Road. The friend was supportive as best she was able.

It quickly became clear, though, that Ann was not keeping her baby safe, and the inevitable happened; her daughter had to be removed into care. All the agencies concerned with Ann were called to a case conference but, for some reason, I was only involved by a telephone call. Following this, it seems that the police arrived at the friend's squat to remove the baby, and told Ann that the lady from the Salvation Army had been responsible for the decision to remove her daughter. Subsequently Ann's drug use and lifestyle became even more chaotic and, of course, she hated me and refused any kind of help.

I can't tell you how betrayed and alone I felt. Already, I'd been overwhelmed with all the suffering, and these latest events made me feel even more separated from God, more of a failure. I knew in my head that this was not possible – God never leaves us or forsakes us, as he promises in Hebrews 13:5 – but that just added guilty feelings to all my other problems.

I was sleepless, exhausted and unable to pray. I was approaching burnout, though I neither recognized this nor knew the name for it. I was going in my own strength and not in God's, a sure recipe for disaster. But the need was so great. I was desperately trying to fill it, to respond, to help, and Ann's situation had brought home to me very forcefully that there was a whole group of people who needed help, and who were not getting it.

There was no service at that time meeting the needs of female sex workers, but there was one afternoon a week when the Candle Project did not open its drop-in. So I approached my boss and asked if I could use the drop-in space on that one vacant afternoon a week, to invite in women who were involved in street-based sex work.

I emphasized that this would not be part of the Candle Project, but rather a personal project. The unsatisfactory opportunity of working with Ann had really impacted me. It broke my heart that she did not have the support she needed to keep her baby, and that she didn't trust me to have her best interests at heart. I hoped that perhaps holding a drop-in might be a first step towards earning the trust of these very vulnerable women.

I managed to recruit three other women to my cause. These women grouped together at what was to become one of my most desperate and futile moments, but they would still become an absolute mainstay of my work and my life for many years.

Sister Annaliese I have already mentioned – the Anglican nun who came to Marcus's funeral with me. Then there was Sister Mary Donnelly, a Catholic nun. She had very recently returned from working in the Zambia, and was coming to live at The Movement for Faith and Justice Today community on Cheltenham Road. In fact, she had only been there for ten minutes when I knocked on the door to talk to the people I knew there about finding me someone to join me in my mission. I didn't even give her time to get her suitcase unpacked – it stood there in the hall as she listened to me unburden myself, saying how much I needed someone to help me run the women's drop-in. It was impetuous and maybe presumptuous of me, but Mary was looking for something – a need and a role – and she said yes. The women would come to love Mary dearly, and she was someone they quickly warmed to. There was something about being an older woman, and being Irish, and just being Mary, that quickly disarmed people and got beyond their defences.

The fourth woman was Dr Dorothy Milne, who had recently retired from her work as a consultant in sexual health at Bristol Royal Infirmary's Milne Centre (named after her when she retired). I had made myself an absolute pain with the Milne Centre medical staff, constantly haranguing them, saying, 'We need your service, we need it, it's brilliant, but we need it where the woman are – not appointments which they don't have a diary for and won't be able to keep . . .' Dorothy evidently found me a useful pain rather than just a pain in the backside.

Another crucial character was Father Raphael Appleby. He was the leader of The Movement for Faith and Justice Today – the ecumenical community of young people in Cheltenham Road. He and I had prayed together a number of times, and he shared my concern for the women selling sex on the streets of our city. He was considering whether The Movement for Faith and Justice Today could offer their premises for this group of marginalized and vulnerable women.

On 12 May 1995 we started meeting in the Candle Project on a Wednesday afternoon between 3.15 p.m. and 6 p.m. We persuaded Bristol Drugs Project and Bristol Health Promotion Service to attend each session for around an hour. We regularly saw six women and their children, and occasionally this would increase to eight or nine. This wasn't enough women to make the project viable, especially for the staff from the drugs and health services, but it still felt worthwhile, and we used this period to try to consolidate our aims and vision.

All seemed to go tentatively well, until a new woman came along to the drop-in one day, and abused our premises terribly by bringing a punter and attempting to use our backyard as a workplace. The credibility we had already been struggling with the Salvation Army to establish was dashed. The project closed.

I had not taken this project to the Lord before starting it. It was a good idea, and something like this was desperately needed, but I had not taken it to God prayerfully. It was not his timing. Crucially, in addition, I was personally not in a fit state to be starting anything new. I felt disillusioned and disappointed when it had to close. I was asking myself the question, 'Where do we go from here?'

This was my first experience of God closing a door. I would experience it again, more than once, in the years to come, but I would also experience God opening doors in miraculous ways.

The project's closure was another sword blow to my heart. I was emotionally exhausted. Meltdown for me came shortly afterwards.

And so we come back to that Tuesday morning Candle drop-in in November 1995. There is the wonderful, blessed bustle of needy people with desperate lives being looked after, even just for an hour or so. They are being provided with enough space and peace to just sit for a while, and let a hot drink warm them and a sandwich fill their belly. People with chaotic lives sitting peacefully in a safe place – somewhere we had provided.

I was at Candle six days a week, I had been leading the women's drop-in on Wednesday evenings then seen it have to close, I was looking after my son, I was going home late and tired to my wonderful husband. It was all too much.

If only I could have just sat there and watched people receiving the love of God in the practical shape of sandwiches and cups of tea. If only I could have enjoyed seeing all these people meeting the love of God where they were at in life, through practical responses to their very real needs. But I was the community manager. I couldn't just sit and observe. I had to stay alert, on the ball.

That's when I noticed Jan go to the toilet, and you know what happened next – the blood, the broken needle, the violence, the mess.

The ambulance had been called. Jan was drugged-up, volatile, violent and aggressive. She was wrecking that medical room – the room I'd sweated blood to provide, and which was so key in getting so many needs seen to. Someone had left the door of that brilliant little room open when they shouldn't have, and Jan was wrecking it, pushing me, spitting. And I was frustrated – frustrated and furious, and so alone. There was blood everywhere and I didn't know what to do. Then she started kicking me.

I was out of control and out of resources. I kicked her back.

This will be to my eternal shame. Me, the community manager, kicking a vulnerable woman who had come to us for help.

The ambulance arrived. The paramedics were brilliant. They knew Jan from previous episodes, and they took her to Bristol Royal Infirmary, where I knew she would receive proper, professional, caring treatment for her immediate needs.

When the ambulance had gone, the other drop-in users melted away outside. The show was over. Everything was quiet. I washed off the blood and spit, as best I could, and I went to see my boss to report on all that had taken place.

I told him everything.

Unsurprisingly, he concluded that I had not handled the situation very well. He said he felt I could not continue managing the project in this way, and sent me home for the rest of the day to reflect on what had happened.

I felt deflated, ashamed, alone and unsupported in my work. This incident was the straw that broke the camel's back. I badly needed a break. I felt revolting and shameful about having kicked Jan. In November 1995, immediately following this incident, I formally requested a sabbatical leave.

I had to wait a month for the response.

I only had to wait a few hours for Jan to reconcile with me. She arrived the following morning, and immediately came to see me. She apologized and gave me a card, saying how sorry she was. I still have that card, to this day. And part of the broken needle is, to my knowledge, still in her foot as the hospital were unable safely to remove it. I apologized too.

It finally came through for me to have three months leave February, March and April 1996. It had been a long and hard five years. I was exhausted physically, mentally, emotionally and spiritually. I had learned a great deal and had a genuine love for the community and the people in it, but ultimately, I had failed. I made it clear to Captain Jones, my boss, that I might not be able to return to work following the sabbatical.

So there I was, at the end of myself. I had failed fundamentally – reacting aggressively and physically to a needy, vulnerable person we should have been helping. The women's drop-in had failed and closed, and I'd messed up at the Candle Project. I couldn't give out any more from my brokenness and heart-ache, even though those had been necessary for me to be fully available to God and to the people I loved. I was empty. God felt a million miles away.

6

Cold Wind, Holy Spirit

I was relieved to have my request for a break accepted. My body was exhausted, my mind was in turmoil and my emotions were wrung out.

I had previously read a book, which now came to mind. *I Hear a Seed Growing*[1] is an inspiring book written by an English woman, Edwina Gateley. Edwina was called by God to go to Chicago and wait for his call. This she did over a period of nine months living in a hermitage in a forest, 'trying to get in touch with myself as a woman, trying to be still and to listen to the God within me.'[2] Well, Edwina listened, and God spoke to her and called her into the city of Chicago to go into the brothels and engage with the prostitutes. I thoroughly recommend reading this book of one woman listening to God and stepping out of the boat.

It is a powerful story and it spoke to me. In January 1996 – waiting for my sabbatical to start – I wrote to Edwina in Genesis House, the Christian safe house she had set up several years previously for female sex workers. I told Edwina that I would shortly have a sabbatical leave and could perhaps be available as a volunteer for a month.

I did not tell her that I was suffering from burnout.

I had a reply from Genesis House very quickly, inviting me to spend the month of March working in their drop-in. They were unable to offer me accommodation and so I asked the Salvation Army Captain if he had any contacts in Chicago. He kindly wrote to a training college which was about a mile from Genesis House and, to my delight, they offered me a small apartment to rent for the month of March.

I spent February 1996 trying to rest at home, not very successfully. Over the previous few months, my confidence and self-esteem had come to an all-time low. I thought I was finished – finished as a community worker, and finished as a Christian. I could not see a way forward. God seemed to be on silent and I felt separated from him. I couldn't make sense of my faith or my connection to God. I could not see any way I could return to work in the St Paul's community, which I loved with all my heart. It was a time of darkness and hopelessness.

In human terms, it was quite crazy to think of going to work as a volunteer in Genesis House. I was exhausted and suffering burnout. Also, it was winter in the windy city – though I was blissfully ignorant at this point as to what a Chicago winter is like. But I somehow knew that this was something I had to do, and Cliff supported me in it.

We purchased my air tickets and on 1 March 1996 Cliff drove me to Heathrow Airport, where my courage failed me. Cliff literally had to push me through security as I was a wreck. In fact, I wept quite a lot of the eight-hour flight and was terrified when I finally landed in Chicago O'Hare International Airport.

I was very kindly met by the principal of the Salvation Army training college and his wife, and they took me through the snow storm to my accommodation in the North Side of the city. The first hurdle was cleared, and how kind it was of them to meet me. The second hurdle was to go out and find somewhere to stock up on food. I was relieved to find a good supermarket within walking distance of my accommodation and so was soon able to have a cup of tea! My flat was safe, comfortable and warm and I was thankful to have it.

Having landed in Chicago on a Saturday afternoon, I spent the remainder of the day just settling in and unpacking. The following morning I went out into the snow and located Genesis House, which was only about a fifteen-minute walk away from my flat.

The building itself was a four-storey detached house on the main road with concrete steps leading up to the front door. The basement was used to store second-hand clothing and supplies, while the ground floor was used as the drop-in. The first floor was used for administration, and the accommodation – for six women – was on the top floor.

At that time in 1996, Chicago had an estimated 64,000 female street-based sex workers. The majority of these women had no safe accommodation and were in poor health due to drug or alcohol abuse. Many were also HIV-positive, as I would later discover.

Having located Genesis House, I wondered what to do with the rest of my day. I decided to have lunch at my flat, and then go for a walk around Lake Michigan. I headed to the shores of the lake, and it was there that I encountered the bitterly cold wind as it blew across the ice of the frozen lake. My head pained with the cold and it soon became clear why nobody else was out for a Sunday afternoon stroll! I was very glad to get back to the warmth of my new home.

I had not expected Chicago to be quite as cold as it turned out to be. It rarely rose above freezing, and I was definitely not dressed appropriately. However, I didn't freeze to death, and my insubstantial clothes, ironically, would become an amusing talking point among the women sex workers!

The instructions which Genesis House had sent over prior to my arrival in Chicago were to arrive at 8 a.m. for the opening of the drop-in. My short walk to work was freezing, but I trembled as much with apprehension as with the cold. I didn't know what I would be expected to do, or whether I would be gratefully received by either staff or drop-in users. It turned out I didn't need to worry about either of these.

Upon my arrival at Genesis House I was greeted by a senior member of staff. 'Thank goodness you have come,' she said. 'Our drop-in manager is off sick. We want you to manage the drop-in today.'

I very quickly explained that I could not manage the drop-in as I too was unwell. 'Yes, but you have experience of managing a drop-in in your own city, and our manager is in hospital.' At this point I should probably have left the building and taken an early flight home. However, in retrospect I am so glad that I stayed.

What happened next, though, unnerved me, and also revealed my inexperience – some might say naïvety. The first person to come through the door of what was a drop-in for women was African-American, very tall, and very glamorously dressed. I greeted them saying that I was a volunteer from England, and giving my name. The person replied in a deep, husky voice, 'My name is Destiny'. It was then that I noticed the very large feet in red high-heeled shoes, and a distinct Adam's apple.

I tried to look cool and said that I needed to check something out with the staff upstairs and that they were welcome to make some coffee – I remember gesturing vaguely as I actually had no idea where the coffee-making equipment was! I ran upstairs and explained that I had a man dressed in female clothing in the women's drop-in, and I wasn't sure what to do. 'Oh yes,' they explained casually. 'That is Dimitri, one of the queens. It's fine.'

'Well, they might have prepared me for that,' I thought.

The second person came a few minutes later – a young African-American woman who looked at me and asked who I was and what was my name.

'My name's Val,' I answered. 'I'm visiting from England.'

She looked at me and simply replied, 'You are really ****ed up, aren't you?'

I replied that I was indeed, and she answered, 'It shows!'

'Oh great,' I thought, ruefully. I had been there all of fifteen minutes and already it was apparent to the women coming in off the streets that I was a mess.

However, that young woman, whose name was Pauline, would become a great friend to me in Chicago, and I shall always be thankful for her honesty and kindness.

The remainder of that day passed finding my way around the building, welcoming newcomers, making coffee and explaining something of myself to the women who came into the drop-in. I need not have been concerned about what they would think of me, as they accepted me for myself and were, on the whole, quite gentle with me. A steady stream of women arrived throughout the day until we closed at 8 p.m. I arrived back at my apartment and prepared my meal, trying to process the events of the day, before enduring a thoroughly sleepless night.

Day two brought more of the same – some of the women who had come the previous day and some new people. I was able to have more in-depth conversations and felt just a little more confident, thinking I might be able to manage, if this was all that was required of me. But silly me! At the end of the day, because I had 'done so well', the staff said I was to spend the following day working in the outreach drop-in on the South Side of Chicago, because the manager there was also sick.

I was informed that I would be picked up by taxi from Genesis House at 8 a.m. the following day. I knew nothing about the South Side of Chicago except for its reputation as the area of social deprivation and violence.

During that night and the early morning of day three, there was a hurricane bringing several feet of snow and closing Chicago O'Hare International Airport. The snow-clearing teams were already busy on the pavements and roads, so I was able to walk to Genesis House through narrow channels in the piled-up drifts. The taxi arrived and I gave him the address. The journey was somewhat illuminating, especially as we drove further into the South Side of the city. Everything became much poorer, with areas of dereliction and lines of homeless people queueing outside of churches for breakfast.

The buildings became fewer and fewer until we drove into an area of total dereliction. At this point the taxi driver stopped and said that this was as far as he was going. I naïvely asked if we had arrived as I couldn't see a building. He replied that if I just kept walking for a couple of blocks, I would come to my address, but repeated that he wasn't going any further.

As I started to walk in the snow and gloom, I noticed there were benders with smoke coming out of them on either side of the road. 'Bender' is the name given to a small, temporary construction made of trees that have been bent over to make a support for waterproof plastic covers to provide shelter – usually for homeless people. I was aware that I was probably being watched, but I could not see a single living person. I strode on, shivering, until I found the only standing building, which was next door to a church that had been barricaded up.

I could hardly believe what I was seeing and getting into. I had gone beyond fear. The house was very much like its sister house on the North Side, being a three-storey house with concrete steps leading to the front door. Sheltering under the steps were three women in insubstantial clothes. I was evidently in the right place.

They greeted me with surprise, wanting to know who I was. They demanded hot coffee even before I had the front door open. They also pointed out the fact that one of the windows of the room, to the right of the front door, had blown in during the previous night's hurricane.

On opening the door, I discovered that the room was full of snow and the triple-glazed window was undamaged but lying on the floor. It was at this point that I realized I needed to take control of the situation. The three women were desperate for coffee, but I took the decision that before anything else, and together, we should clear the snow out of the room and secure the window back in its place.

In spite of loud complaints, we gathered a washing-up bowl and saucepans and shovelled the snow out of the window. All four of us then, somehow, lifted the heavy window and, struggling, managed to get it back into its frame. It didn't help that the three other women were more than a little unsteady on their feet – probably due to drug intake as well as high-heeled shoes. But we did it, and I had established some authority.

Their reward was to make themselves breakfast, which they assured me they were normally allowed to do. I still have no idea if this was correct, but they and I were all in need of food and coffee. And so, following a delicious fried breakfast cooked by my three new friends, one of whom turned out to be Pauline from my first day, we faced the day . . .

And what a day it proved to be! I was in sole charge of a service I knew nothing about, in a country where I didn't belong, the day after a hurricane had wreaked havoc! I quickly allocated jobs for the three women already there, so they could help me run the drop-in – making hot drinks, finding and allocating clothing and other necessities to give to those in need, serving food, generally keeping an eye on everyone and 'policing' the drop-in.

There was a constant stream of women arriving all day. They were cold, hungry and needed warm clothing, drinks and food. They were all, to varying degrees, under the influence of drugs (crack cocaine being the drug of choice) and this made them unpredictable, demanding and subject to dramatic mood swings in short spaces of time. It was frantic, but somehow immensely rewarding, and my three friends were brilliant. We somehow got right through the day – 8 a.m. to 8 p.m. – a twelve-hour shift, and I was ready to drop. However, it was not over yet – not by a long way.

Having no idea how I would be able to return to the safety of my apartment on the other side of the city, in the dark and at night, I had planned to sleep on one of the sofas at the drop-in and then make my way back to Genesis House in daylight the following morning. However, as we were clearing up at the end of the day, one of the original women, Josephine, told me that we were not closing at 8 p.m., as this was the evening on which they had their weekly PA meeting.

'What's a PA meeting?' I enquired. Josephine told me PA stood for Prostitutes Anonymous. This was not something I had come across before. Several of the women went into the basement of the house to prepare the room for the meeting and were shortly joined by around a dozen other women coming in from the street. The usual coffee was prepared and after I had checked that they had everything they needed, I returned upstairs to make myself a cup of tea.

Within a few minutes, Josephine came upstairs and invited me to join the meeting. She explained that this was very unusual as I was not a sex worker, and that absolute confidentiality was expected of me. I accepted the invitation and joined them.

That meeting changed my life.

One by one, those remarkable and courageous women stood up and shared their stories. They would begin with the words, 'I am [Josephine]. I am a prostitute and a drug addict.' Many added, 'and I'm HIV-positive.' They would then share something of where they were at in life, and on the road out of addiction and homelessness. Many tears were shed, by them and by me. A few of those present were no longer sex workers and had mostly overcome their drug habit. They attended for support for themselves, and to offer hope to those still struggling. It was a thoroughly moving and humbling experience.

Most of the women spoke of having had their children removed into social care and of feeling there was little hope of ever regaining control of their lives because of the drug and homelessness issues. In spite of this, each one had dignity and spoke words of truth. They knew exactly where they were at. There was no pretence.

They also appeared to have faith in God – a God of mercy, the God who was with them on the streets, as they struggled to build new lives for themselves. It blew my mind, and to tell the truth, I felt envious of their faith. Still today, all these years later, I feel privileged and honoured to have been invited into that meeting.

Around 10 p.m., as the last of the women left the building, I was left with Pauline. What a treasure Pauline turned out to be. She realized that I didn't have a clue about how to return to the North Side of the city, and that it was dark, dangerous and also very cold. She offered to accompany me back to the elevated train service known as the Loop, which operates in Chicago. I gladly accepted her offer and we set off to walk through this notorious neighbourhood, so foreign and potentially threatening to me.

I felt safe in the company of Pauline, and we chatted about our lives as we walked. She travelled with me all the way to the nearest Loop station, close by Genesis House, where she knew I could make my way home. I shall always be thankful for her kindness in delivering me back to within walking distance of my flat. Sadly, Pauline then returned to the streets to work, leaving my heart aching for her and the other women I had shared the day with.

I spent Thursday, my fourth day in Genesis House, working in the drop-in again, but as the day went on, I was aware of a growing weariness in my spirit. I returned to my flat that evening exhausted emotionally, physically and spiritually. I fell to my knees and cried out loud in desperation, my only prayer for months.

'God! Help me!'

Again and again I cried out to him, in anguish and desperation – 'God! Help me!' I cried – buckets of tears, baths of tears, months' and months' worth of tears that had built up inside me. And still I called out, 'God! Help me!'

I have no idea how long I was there on the floor – it could have been minutes, or hours, but it was there that God met me. There was nowhere else to go, and no one else to go to. It was just me and God. Out poured all my sadness, frustration, anger and heartbreak. And God, in his mercy and grace, met me there in my brokenness.

After a time, I physically felt God's hands on my shoulders, lifting me, picking me up off the floor. I sat on a chair, and I cried out to him to forgive me and to take me to a new place. I was wracked with sobs and exhausted from the crying. I wanted to be broken – to be at the end of my self-reliance – and I longed for a new, deeper relationship with the God of Life.

7

Jesus in Jail

Later that evening as I was eating my supper, I remembered a conversation I'd had with a Christian leader back in Bristol. Dave Day was the senior pastor in Bristol Christian Fellowship, and he had given me some wise words of advice when I first realized I was falling apart, and had applied for my sabbatical. Then, when he discovered I was coming to Chicago, he had mentioned that he and a team from his church would be in Madison, Wisconsin, that same weekend, to deliver some teaching. Dave had said that if I needed help, I should ring him in Madison.

The next day – a Friday morning – I rang the number Dave had given me from the phone at Genesis House. Dave listened to my cry for help and told me to book a flight that evening to Madison. He said that he would meet me at the airport, and I could join the team as an observer. Dave also said that Bristol Christian Fellowship would pay for my flights as he was aware that I had little money available.

I duly booked the flight and as soon as I was able to leave the drop-in, late in the afternoon, I made my way to O'Hare International Airport. The flight to Madison only took an hour and I arrived to join the team just as they were about to enjoy pizza in the home of the Madison pastor they were with. Although I knew several members of the team from Bristol, I was unable to join in and kept myself apart as much as possible, so as not to invite questions or conversation which I knew I could not handle. Later that evening, we drove to a Bible camp alongside a frozen lake, which was the meeting place for the weekend.

Here, I met members of the Madison church who were attending the teaching weekend, as we shared hot chocolate before bed. Again, I kept myself separate in the knowledge that I would not be able to handle even the most basic questions as to who I was and what I was doing there.

Saturday morning arrived and it was a bright and very cold day. After breakfast, the Bristol team and I went for a walk on the frozen lake. It was beautiful and a new experience for me, walking on a frozen lake. It gave me a little boost of nature-inspired adrenalin. Amazing. We went back to the centre and the teaching began after coffee. Different sessions took place throughout the day and I sat at the back, listening and observing.

Sunday morning was another bright day and the teaching started immediately after breakfast. There were lots of prayer opportunities during the day but I did not ask for prayer. I had noticed, though, that there was an older man who, like me, did not take part in the various sessions. He too sat at the back alone. It was during Sunday afternoon as I was thinking about my return to Chicago that evening, and not knowing how I would be able to continue, that this man approached me.

He said he had noticed that I appeared to be depressed and not to be taking part, and asked if he could pray for me. I somewhat reluctantly agreed, and I am so glad that I did. He shared that he was a retired surgeon and was somewhat 'on the edge' of the Christian community, but that God had spoken very clearly to him telling him to pray with me. We sat next to each other and he prayed.

I have no idea what he prayed, but the result was a quite miraculous lifting of the oppression and weariness I had been experiencing. It was amazing, and instantaneous. I felt strengthened, filled up with God's goodness, comforted, healed and joyful again. The space created by everything I'd poured out the night before was now brimming over with a Holy Spirit-given warmth and confidence. Incredible!

I am to this day very grateful to that man. He heard God asking him to pray for me, and he was obedient – and compassionate. What a difference it made! His prayers set me off on a whole new path. The necessary breaking had made way for restoration and renewal, and I knew that I could now continue for the remainder of my time in Chicago.

I am very grateful to Dave Day and the team from Bristol Christian Fellowship for their generosity and kindness at that time. I learned some years later that they had in fact been quite concerned about me as I appeared to be on the brink of a nervous breakdown. They made themselves available to support me, and God brought me back from that brink.

Sunday evening was the time for me to return to Chicago and I somewhat reluctantly said goodbye to my friends from Bristol. I had an uneventful short flight to O'Hare but was totally confused on arrival as how to get out of the airport and find a taxi. In my confusion, I was on the wrong level and left the building from Arrivals, but I was quite unaware of this.

Almost immediately, a taxi drew up and as the passengers left the car, I threw my bag on the back seat. The driver at once told me that I could not get in the car as this was the Arrivals level and that I should go down to Departures to catch a taxi. I replied, 'I am not getting out, please drive me down to Departures and we can go from there.' The driver laughed and did just that.

I think because the cab driver could see that I was a complete novice at all this, he chatted during the journey telling me how he had arrived from India just a year previously with his wife and was also finding his way around. It was a small, unexpected blessing for my return journey, and he was great company on the way back to Chicago.

I returned to Genesis House and had yet more truly life-changing experiences. One of these was to go on outreach to Cook County Jail to meet women who had been arrested the previous evening for soliciting. The wonderful arrangement Genesis House had with the county court was that, dependent upon space being available, if a sex-working woman showed motivation for change, she could be bailed to the safe house, rather than kept in jail.

I arrived at the prison having been given a bunch of leaflets about the scheme, but unclear as to what I was supposed to do there. I was taken by a warder through the prison to a large cell, which had fourteen women in it. The warder said gruffly that he would collect me in two hours' time. I turned to reply that I would not need two hours, but the cell door closed and I was inside.

There was a slotted seat attached to the wall around three sides of the room and an open stainless-steel toilet in a corner, where one woman was being sick. Two women were fighting, loudly encouraged by some of the others. I realized these women would have been high on drugs when arrested, and would now be in the process of withdrawing – this explained their agitation.

I decided to sit down on the seat, and was immediately offered a roll-up, which I declined as I don't smoke. It was at this point that I realized the women thought I was the oldest hooker in town!

I tried to open up a conversation, remembering why I was there, and they straight away picked up the fact that I was English. I explained that I was a volunteer from England working in Genesis House. At this point they all gathered around asking questions such as 'Do you know Lady Di?' to which I replied that I did not.

Over the time I was there, they all calmed down quite a bit, and became delightful company. The two women fighting stopped and joined in the conversation. One of them named Magnolia said that it was her fortieth birthday, and asked me to sing 'Happy Birthday' to her. We all joined together to sing to Magnolia, and there was laughter at my attempt at outreach. And, would you believe it, one of those arrested the previous evening was Pauline, of whom I have already spoken. Pauline had been bailed to Genesis House and I would spend time with her there on her arrival later that day and in the days to come.

The time in that cell flew by. The women were curious as to why I was there in Chicago and they assumed that I had worked with the prostitute women in my home city. They were surprised and pleased that I had gone to their city to learn more about them. A few of them shared their stories and there was a general sense of togetherness and calm.

When the warder arrived two hours later, we were all in the middle of the cell with our arms around each other's shoulders as they asked me to pray for each one. There were lots of tears but also joy as we shared together. It was another life-changing experience. I still remember the look of astonishment on the face of the warder when he opened the door to the cell. He clearly had not expected to see a group of women huddled together, praying!

Whenever I think back to that occasion, and my total inadequacy for the job I was meant to be doing, two things stand out. The first is that God was present with those women in the cell and with me on that March morning. The second is the acceptance those women had for a stranger who was clearly vulnerable, if not floundering. I was accepted for who I was, at face value, and I was welcomed.

I was about to meet Edwina Gateley during my second week in Chicago. Edwina was no pushover. She had completely forgotten that I was coming and wanted to know who I was and what I was capable of. She gave me the task of washing all the walls in Genesis House – 'All of them,' she emphasized. There were four floors of rooms with walls. I was inwardly furious. Didn't she know that I was the community manager in a busy drop-in back home in Bristol? But no, I had to prove my worth there and then, so I got on with the task.

Then, Edwina told me that she had an important trustees' meeting later that day, and gave me the task of cooking an English meal for sixteen people, which included six Genesis House residents and myself. The choice of meal was mine. That morning, Genesis House had received a donation of potatoes and cooking apples that were fallers, and so I had some ingredients to start with. I decided upon cottage pie with vegetables, followed by apple crumble and custard. I took one of the residents with me to the supermarket and we purchased meat, carrots and cabbage.

The tricky bit came when I announced to the residents that they would need to help me peel the potatoes and apples. This was not something they would normally do, and I had lots of complaints. However, I wielded my new-found confidence, and insisted. We produced a delicious English meal which we presented to Edwina and the trustees, and then sat down and enjoyed with them.

My four weeks of working in Genesis House were always challenging. Every day presented a new learning opportunity! It is generally accepted that the UK often experiences trends several years later than they take hold in the US. This was definitely the case with crack cocaine, which has had devastating effects in both countries, on individuals and communities. I saw this first-hand in Chicago in 1996 – how men and women who already had a drug problem with heroin were drawn further into the madness and sickness of having two addictions – crack cocaine and heroin. Crack to give them a high, and heroin to bring them down. Both leading to death of the human spirit and the physical body. Crack cocaine hit the UK in the latter half of the nineties.

The Chicago Drugs Alliance had an arrangement with Genesis House to provide a worker to go on their outreach van once a week. This took place on a Thursday between 10 a.m. and twelve noon and then between 2 p.m. and 4 p.m. I was sent once again to the South Side to join the Drugs Alliance team for this outreach. I met them at their depot at 9 a.m. to prepare the van, which was huge. We loaded three empty wheelie bins onto the van, together with boxes full of new needles, and small containers of clean water.

The team consisted of a driver, a worker to get the ramp down from the side of the van to the pavement and manage the number of people entering the van, a counsellor who was positioned at the rear of the van in a small area to the side, and me to count in used needles and give clean needles in return. Another ramp was positioned at the rear to enable people to leave the van in a smooth flow.

We drove to our first stop of the morning, which was the Vietnam Veterans Hospital. My job was simply to count in the used needles – which were placed on a narrow counter in front of me – and in return to provide the same number of clean needles plus an extra ten. There were often fifty or so dirty needles to be counted in per person. The idea of giving an increased number of needles back was to encourage them to use clean needles for their drug use, and not to share with other users. This is essential in reducing the risk of HIV and hepatitis.

At 10 a.m. on the dot, men started to come out of the hospital and queue to come onto the van. Many of these men were in wheelchairs, having lost limbs. It was a truly wretched sight. Each person was clutching a black bin liner containing their used needles, which they placed on the counter, and as I counted they pushed them into the wheelie bins. I then gave them their clean needles. Few words were spoken but I tried to smile at each person and treat each with respect and acceptance. But the degree of human brokenness I witnessed was both sad and depressing. The whole of the first session – two hours – was spent at the Vietnam Veterans Hospital, as the men came in the front of the van and left at the rear. Quite a number spent time with the counsellor and about half, I think, had lost limbs, either as a result of warfare, or through drug use.

We drove off at noon and headed to McDonald's for lunch. I had no appetite at all. The break, though, gave me the opportunity to talk with members of the team, who were lovely people and very caring. The second session of the day started at 2 p.m. and ended at 4 p.m., but was not as distressing as the morning had been. We moved around the streets and both men and women accessed the service. At the end of the day, when we drove back to the Drugs Alliance depot, we unloaded the three large wheelie bins of used needles. Each bin was full to the brim. It was truly sickening, and I know that God's heart ached for each of those people, as did mine.

The Saturday following my experience on the Drugs Alliance van, I had a lovely surprise. At nine o'clock in the morning, my doorbell rang and it was Pauline! She invited me to join her on a 'sightseeing day' that she had planned for me in Chicago. I gladly accepted and what a day that was – not the usual visitors' experience of sightseeing the posh and glitzy, but a glimpse of Pauline's city.

It was memorable, and a day of yet more unusual experiences – some of which left me with questions hanging in my mind. I met some of her friends, male and female, and we ate together in a few dingy cafés, where the food was cheap but good. It was all very natural and although one of us was a support worker and one a service user, there was no distinction between the two of us. We were just two women enjoying each other's company, chatting and sharing our lives.

The remainder of my time working in the drop-in was spent engaging with the women over coffee. In addition, I spent a few days doing what I had done on a number of occasions in Bristol – cleaning! Genesis House had a move-on apartment which had been badly used and needed cleaning – top to bottom. It took three of us several days to clean the two-bed apartment thoroughly and safely dispose of drug paraphernalia.

I learned so much during my month in Chicago – about myself, about God, and about the lives of women enslaved by drug and alcohol abuse and prostitution. During my last week, the residents and staff in Genesis House all told me that I needed to be working with the women on the streets of Bristol. I think I knew this in my heart, but I had no idea as to how to make it happen – though I did by now know that I shouldn't try to make it happen, but must seek God for how to do it.

I also had the opportunity to talk to Edwina Gateley when she visited the house during my last week. Edwina encouraged me to spend time with God seeking the way forward. I knew in my heart that my time in the Candle Project was coming to an end, but I doubted my ability to begin a new charity at the age of 55 years, with no money and only a little experience of working with sex-working women.

My last day arrived. I had said goodbye to Genesis House, and spent the morning cleaning the flat and packing. Around midday I received a visit from the wife of the principal of the Salvation Army Training College. She invited me to lunch with the students and later to visit one of their hostels for homeless men. I accepted, but was somewhat disappointed to learn that they had no knowledge of Genesis House and the amazing work undertaken there. Genesis House was, after all, only a mile away. The visit to the men's hostel and drop-in was interesting and I was invited by the manager to participate in the activities and talk to some of the residents. It was an excellent facility.

My flight home was late evening and a member of Genesis House staff had offered to drive me to the airport. When they arrived, I was delighted to see that they were driving me in a minivan, and that six of the residents had come along in the van to see me off! I had a wonderful, if somewhat noisy, send-off with lots of hugs and tears on my part. But I was going home to my lovely husband and I longed to be with him again. I also needed to share with Cliff that we – he and I – might be about to start on a new adventure!

My time in Chicago was pivotal in my growth as a Christian and as a woman. I had arrived there broken, depressed and doubting that I could ever again work with people on the margins of our society. A large part of this was knowing that I had abused a vulnerable woman by kicking her. Regardless of the fact that she had kicked me first, I was horrified and shocked that I had been capable of such behaviour, even under duress, and had found it difficult to forgive myself.

In Genesis House, and in Cook County Jail, I found acceptance. The prostitute women I worked with didn't judge me or expect anything of me. Instead, they gave what they had to me – acceptance of who I was at that time, no questions, no judgement. I saw Jesus in those women, in the same way I'd seen Jesus in the faces of some of the men and women I had worked with in Bristol.

I saw Jesus in their unswerving honesty, their refusal to hide behind niceties. I found freedom in their wholehearted, straightforward acceptance of me, imperfections and all. Their love for me, their unconditional acceptance, their welcome of me, was just like his. In this way, the people I was serving and working with, and meeting the needs of, became part of my salvation. They had shown me Jesus.

When I set off back to Bristol I was changed. I was stronger – in God and in myself, secure in my faith. I was also certain of what I needed to do. Gone was the sense of failure and guilt, and gone also was the desperate activity, the energy-sapping frantic exertion. This was replaced with a desire to understand the reasons why women were out there on the street, and how they could be reached.

The women at Genesis had expressed concern that there was not an agency in Bristol working with female sex workers, and they had encouraged me to go back home and set one up. I couldn't see how, but I was willing.

Sadly, Genesis House closed several years ago due to lack of funding. What a huge loss to the sex workers and to the city of Chicago. Being a small part of Genesis House was an informative and transformative time in my life and – even more importantly – it would soon be shaping my future.

8

Cigarettes, Condoms and Saggy Chins

I spent the month of April, the last month of my sabbatical, processing all that had taken place in Chicago, and just appreciating being home in the spring. Cliff and I had a memorable day trip to the National Trust garden of Hidcote, where the spring flowers were so beautiful, and nourished my soul.

The transition back from the pain and suffering I had witnessed in Chicago was something I had to work through. Through my work at Genesis House, I had known both pain and joy, and these are often closely related in our lives. This was also brought home to me when a dear friend of mine, Pat, died during the last week of March.

I had spent time with Pat before going away. We had both known that it might be our final meeting, and on that day, Pat had asked me to lead her funeral. I had only once led a funeral before. Pat had chosen her hymns, and we had discussed the array of different people and groups who would be present at the service, from a range of different scenarios in Pat's life.

Pat and I had climbed mountains together in Austria and eaten delicious Austrian ice cream. We had gone on to laugh, cry and share our lives together over a number of years. Now I was leading her friends and family in this part of grief's journey – remembering her with joy even as we mourned. What a privilege for a friend.

On reflection, I realized that burnout had crept up on me over a period of time working in the Candle Project. Sadness, grief and disappointment were all factors leading to my eventual breakdown – and yes, it was a breakdown. My heart had been breaking as men and women died, sometimes alone and on the street. They were lost, but so, in a sense, was I.

I had been exhausted in mind, body and spirit and was no longer functioning in a sensible way. I had been giving out while unable to receive – a recipe for disaster. The joy had gone out of working with these needy people, and I could only see the problems.

It is absolutely essential for workers like me to have regular supervision, where they are able to offload their anxieties and disappointments, and discuss the way forward in a confidential environment. This should be paid for by their employer, and should be provided by a trained counsellor outside of the organization.

Later on, when I started working in a new project with female sex workers in Bristol that became known as One25 Ltd, I promised God and myself that I would not allow such breakdown to happen again – to me or anyone else. I took better care of myself and had regular supervision and retreats. Being in the wild places such as Dartmoor or walking in Cumbria or Scotland became much more important to me (just like the frozen lake I'd walked on, in Madison County). It was in these places of beauty and isolation that I reconnected to my inner self and communed with God. I could breathe deeply and restore my sense of peace and connection.

I also started having regular spiritual direction, which has been helpful over the years, particularly at times of difficulty. A spiritual director is a trained listener who gives you space and encourages you to talk about your spiritual journey. They reflect back and help you process what's going on, then they work with you to plot a course through the next phase of your spiritual life.

Coming home to Cliff was wonderful, as was coming back to our home, which was ordered and well-kept. Throughout the following years, Cliff would often be running me a bath when I came home from some of the most difficult days. Having flowers in the house, and beautiful toiletries, and order, were some of the simple things which kept me sane and whole while I was giving out to others.

Do I regret that the burnout and breakdown happened? Strangely enough, no. I realize that without it I probably would not have faced the fact that I was drifting spiritually, and had lost my God-given focus. The experience of brokenness and feeling separated from God was excruciatingly painful but, in retrospect, a precious gift.

I came back from Chicago a different person. I had regained my confidence and was no longer a wreck. I knew that my time at the Candle Project was over, and that I needed to work with women like the ones I'd met in Chicago. God had laid them on my heart, I can honestly say that.

In April I also time spent talking to Sister Annaliese, of the Community of the Sisters of the Church. She shared my concern, and was a key member of the emerging group to work with sex-working women. However, she was already in full-time ministry in her community, providing food, shelter and comfort to needy people and families in St Paul's.

As well as Annaliese, I also communicated with Dorothy and Mary about how the project should move forward. We all wanted something to happen – but we were being realistic about how much commitment each person could give, and what the different roles would be.

If the women's drop-in project were to re-start, I thought, it would be under God's guidance, and I would be doing it prayer-fully, patiently, with support and proper self-management – and without doing 100 other things at the same time.

Cliff and I spent many hours in prayer and discussion. We agreed that my time at the Candle Project was at an end, and I wrote my letter of resignation. I would return for the month of May to work my notice.

Then, rather than trying to juggle everything myself, it was agreed that I would commit to working full-time as the pro-ject development worker in our new women's drop-in project. Unpaid.

This was a major step of faith in several ways. There was no money for the project. In order to apply for grants, or other funding, it is necessary to have charitable status, and that was some way down the line. So I would have no salary at all. Cliff would be funding the entire project! We still had a mortgage on our home. Cliff and I talked and decided that paying the mortgage had to take precedence over other bills in order to keep a roof over our heads. Each month we carefully managed Cliff's salary in order to fund the new project, and run our home, and we prayed and trusted that God would provide.

There were occasions when, having put money aside for the mortgage, we were short on paying, for example, an electric-ity bill. And, lo and behold, an anonymous donation would be pushed through our door with almost the exact amount we needed. We never once went into debt, and we never asked friends or family for help. We were always provided for – miraculously.

As well as the lack of funding, I was very aware that I still knew little about working with women involved in sex work. I would need to start carefully and patiently, and involve people and organizations who had more expertise than myself. I would need to learn what was needed, and how best to meet the need. Personally, I don't always think things through – that's not my natural way of being. I'm a visionary, but I'm not a strategic thinker. It drives me crazy when I hear people analysing things, I just think, 'For goodness' sake, just get on and do it!' I would need to hold this side of my personality back for a little while!

The group of four – myself, Dr Dorothy Milne and Sisters Annaliese and Mary – discussed the need to form a consultative group involving professionals working in the area of health and drugs. We invited members from the Department of Genito Urinary Medicine in the Milne Centre of the Bristol Royal Infirmary along with representatives from Bristol Health Promotion Service and Bristol Drugs Project to join us to form policies and share expertise. This group would meet over a period of eighteen months to guide the formation of the project.

I had made some contacts with these organizations during my time at the Candle Project. Most memorably, during a multi-agency meeting, I had met a beautiful female outreach worker who worked for Bristol Drugs Project and went on outreach several nights each week, taking clean needles to known chaotic drug users. Clara invited me to accompany her on a couple of occasions. She told me to wear strong footwear, preferably boots, and to be prepared to climb into squats through windows.

Clara appeared to show no fear and calmly and confidently appraised the situation she was stepping into. It was also obvious that she was trusted by everyone she visited. Clara though, was not foolhardy – she was fully aware of her surroundings and watchful of the possibilities of danger. I learned much from her during those few evenings that would stand me in good stead for future work.

We met at 125 Cheltenham Road, the property owned by The Movement for Faith and Justice Today, with Father Raphael. They allowed us to use the building without charge, and had also installed a kitchen and shower unit, which made it an ideal location for the possible women's drop-in, in the future.

We wanted to know that we were providing a service that was needed and wanted by the women we aimed to reach – not something which we presumed they needed, or which was convenient for us. I devised a questionnaire, and with it I took to the streets to ask female sex workers what would help them. I also took a flask of hot chocolate and a packet of cigarettes, and I hit the streets of night-time St Paul's.

I knew a few of the women on the streets from my time working in the Candle Project, so I started with them. Others, upon seeing that these women were happy to speak to me, also responded. I tried to be quick, efficient and respectful – these women were at work, and would suffer if I took up too much of the time they could have spent earning.

The women unanimously responded that their main need was for a women-only safe space they could go to. It was confirmation that we were on the right track. At that stage, the idea of a women-only drop-in service was new and untested.

Indeed, I later learned that there was only one other similar project starting in the country, and that was in Hackney, London.

In June 1996, we opened in the basement of 125 Cheltenham Road as a once-a-week drop-in for women selling sex from the street. We had asked the women we had contact with what we should officially call ourselves and they had suggested together that it be known simply as '125' as this sounded anonymous to anyone listening, especially to any pimps or boyfriends. We played briefly with numbers and letters, and decided upon One25 as the name of our developing charity.

Upon reflection, all these years later, I still ask myself how best to refer to the women we worked with. We have generally used 'sex worker', as a term which is accurate, and non-judgemental. The truth is that they are women, and should not be given a label which stigmatises them. It is too easy to miss the fact that these are vulnerable people who are very often being exploited. They are somebody's daughter, sister, or mother. They are simply women.

The irony is that the women themselves generally used the word 'prostitute' to describe who they were and what they did. They called a spade a spade. They weren't interested in dressing anything up in respectable words. They just wanted to be seen.

Very few women came to the weekly evening drop-in at first, but we attracted one very interesting woman who worked in the city hotels and was on a bleeper – so that the hotel could contact her if they had a client for her.

Anita came to almost every session. She was a little older than most of the woman, but immensely beautiful and attractive. She took care of herself, and took it upon herself to 'educate' us in various ways. She had us hanging upside down over the back of chairs in order to reduce our sagging chins, and also shared with us about her own experiences as a working girl. This proved to be quite challenging morally, because she did not fit the mould of a powerless, put-upon sex worker. Neither was she a cold, damaged woman who could divorce her feelings from her work. Her attitude to her work was professional on the whole, but for some of her regular clients, she displayed feelings of care or even tenderness.

We learned much from Anita. Some of it was how to keep our bodies toned and youthful. Some of it was how to deal with dynamics that sent our moral compasses into a spin.

I described this to my supervisor. I said, 'Anita messes with my head.' We rely sometimes on rigid moral frameworks to sort and process our experience of other people – we sort them into 'doing the right thing' or 'not doing the right thing'. This is natural, but sometimes these frameworks fall short, as they did for me with Anita.

To deal with this, either we tend to close down to that person, cutting off relationship, or we deny the complexity of their situation, or we abandon our moral framework. None of those things work, and it can mean that Christians find it particularly hard to relate to people with chaotic lives.

If we can find a way to live with the tensions, to accept and love that person, to continue relating to them even though we cannot even form a personal opinion on whether they are doing the 'right' thing or not, then something amazing can happen. We can learn, love and give according to their need, and according to God's unconditional love, and we will be treating them with a dignity that can often be absent from situations we find morally cut and dried.

This is something I continue to learn – it's not easy. But I know that if I can do it, I will be a more generous-hearted person, better able to help and show Jesus' love, and also more adept at supporting someone who has decided that they want to change and move on in their life.

We had a few regulars, like Anita, who valued our service immensely, but on the whole, the numbers coming to the drop-in at 125 Cheltenham Road remained low. This appeared to be due to the fact that it was just off the working beat and was therefore away from the main working area for the women. In order to come, they would need to cross the A38, a major road, and spend quite a bit of time away from work – which had financial implications.

The women are not out there for fun. For the most part, they are out there because they have a drug habit, or because their boyfriend or pimp has a drug habit. So they need to earn sometimes hundreds of pounds in a day. When you consider that the average punter won't be paying much more than £20, you can see the issue.

Building on my time with the questionnaire, I started doing a regular outreach to the women on the streets – going to them, rather than hoping they would come to us. I went in the evenings, to areas where I knew they were working. I took a rucksack with hot chocolate, some bars of chocolate and condoms.

I should add here that the condoms were paid for by my husband. One thousand a month, if you please, were delivered to our home in Cliff's name! I had written to two suppliers to ask for a free supply, but these were not forthcoming. Cliff funded everything we needed in the first two and a half years of One25. I was working from home because, although

The Movement for Faith and Justice Today provided their basement for the drop-in, it couldn't be used as an office, or as a business address.

I also always had a packet of cigarettes in my pocket, and these proved to be an easy way to start a conversation. We had a policy that stated we could offer cigarettes to the women, and I was immensely grateful for this. Obviously, cigarettes are not a healthy option, but in the context of a drug-addicted, chaotic life, with the ever-present threat of HIV from clients, or from needles, a cigarette was the least of anyone's worries. Interestingly, it was in fact Dorothy – the retired medical consultant – who provided the cigarettes.

I would start the conversation by telling the women that I was part of a new project working with female sex workers, and would explain what the drop-in offered. I also asked them what we could provide that would help them – in fact, I sometimes took my original questionnaire. Again, the majority answered that a women-only safe space was what they needed. But the numbers at the drop-in remained low.

Sister Mary, Dorothy, Sister Annaliese and myself could see that we needed to be 'out there' with the women in a more realistic way. But how would we do this? The professional drug and health workers quite reasonably decided that we were not attracting enough women into the drop-in to make it feasible for them to continue their support. We needed to rethink our approach. That was, perhaps, the first major lesson I learned when working with this marginalized group of women – the need to be constantly assessing the work and responding flexibly.

We kept the drop-in going for eighteen months at 125 Cheltenham Road, and although few women accessed our help, this was still a valuable time of training for our group of committed volunteers – now sixteen people. Without the support and encouragement of these valuable volunteer women, it would have been difficult to keep going and plan for the future of the project. It was also valuable for me doing my foot outreach in the area as I slowly got to know a few women and built quite solid relationships.

Interestingly, it was during this time of foot outreach that the pimps and boyfriends who were controlling the women also got to know and accept me. Indeed, on one occasion I was approached by a man I knew to be a pimp. He asked me to go around the corner to a new woman who needed a hot drink and some condoms! I was taken aback by his cheek, but I did as he asked, and established contact with a woman who was new to the city.

We would continue to build a relationship of trust with that particular woman, and it would eventually lead to her breaking free from both drug abuse and sex working, but it took many years. Working with women involved in the sex industry is a long haul. There are few quick fixes.

In June 1997, exactly a year since One25 started, during my quiet time one evening, I brought before God our need for something else to enable us to reach more women, safely. The thought came into my mind of a van, and so I asked God for a van please. 'Before the winter,' I added.

During that week I was invited to speak to a small group of ladies from a local church who had heard about One25. I shared with them my prayer for a van. In human terms this was quite crazy as we had no money at all apart from one very dubious £5 note. (It had been pressed into my hand when I was on outreach one evening by a local man whose flat the women sometimes used for business – upon payment. Another moral labyrinth.)

Exactly a week later, there was a knock on our front door in the evening. Cliff answered the door to a man we'd never met before, who asked if Val Jeal lived there. Cliff called me and stayed with me as the man introduced himself as the pastor of Cornerstone Ministries, a local free church. 'I have been praying,' he said, 'and God has told me you need a van . . .'

9

The Custard Van

It must have been quite comical to see Cliff and me as our mouths fell open in astonishment, but this wonderful man simply handed over a logbook, making a gift to us of a Ford Transit van. He gave me the name of a member of his congregation to ring the following day to make all the arrangements. At that moment I remember thinking that the sky might fall in, such was my astonishment.

The following day, I duly rang Mike Ogborne, the man in Cornerstone Ministries whose name I had been given, and I was invited over immediately to look at the van. It was elderly but in good working condition. It was fitted with seats to carry passengers, but Mike asked if we would like these seats removed in order to rearrange the space in a different way. As I looked at the interior of the van, I could see that what we needed would be two bench seats, running along either side of the van, front to back. Mike said he could do this. I then asked if we could have some cupboards with worktops fitted behind the driver's cab in order to store food items and make drinks. Mike agreed to this also. And then, wonderfully, Mike said that the van had an up-to-date MOT and was taxed for the next eleven months, and that Cornerstone would sign it over to us. It was absolutely amazing! An answer to prayer within a week, and generosity such as I had never expected or experienced.

The van was white and Mike asked how I felt about that. I replied that it would be wonderful if it could be yellow. Again, Mike agreed to paint the van and I chose a bright yellow colour. I can't explain why it had to be yellow, but I just knew that it should. All of the work was paid for by Cornerstone Ministries. A wonderful and generous gift that really blew me away.

About a week later Mike rang me to say that the van was ready to be collected. Cornerstone had also agreed that we could continue to park the van on their premises, which was a real gift.

The next problem was insuring a van for use on outreach to female sex workers. I rang a number of insurance companies and hedged around the van's use – it would be used for outreach to women, I said, some of whom were homeless. Yes, came the reply, what kind of women? I then had to come clean and say that the women we wanted to reach were female sex workers. All of the insurance companies refused cover at that point.

Eventually, I found one insurance company who specialized in providing cover for Christian churches and other religious projects. Hopeful, I telephoned them, and they also refused.

At this point I was frustrated and not a little angry. I found myself saying crossly to the person on the other end of the telephone that I would write to *The Guardian* newspaper exposing their hypocrisy in refusing insurance to a charity with a Christian ethos working with marginalized women. They rang back about fifteen minutes later and offered to insure the van, but at a very high premium – just short of £1,000. I accepted, gratefully, but with no idea how we would raise the money.

In the past, at the Candle Project, I had done a lot of public speaking at churches and in women's groups about the need for help to work with homeless men and women in Bristol. The help we received then was both generous and encouraging, and so I turned again to this method of fundraising and awareness-raising. I approached several local churches and asked if it might be possible for me to come along and share about One25. Once again, people responded with great generosity, both financially and in volunteering to work with us. By September 1997 I had the money to insure the van.

I had never before driven a Ford Transit van and so I enlisted the help of one of our faithful volunteers, Hazel, who had experience of driving vans in her work with the NHS. And so it was that one September evening Hazel and I, together with Hazel's dog, took the van into St Paul's for me to learn the ropes. Hazel drove well. I was not so good, and the lesson was memorable for all the wrong reasons.

I was trying to be subtle, and to concentrate on driving this enormous vehicle safely. But keeping a low profile in a bright, custard-yellow transit van is not easy. I kept seeing men I knew from the Candle Project, who would recognize me, point and laugh, or shout questions about what I was doing driving a big van around St Paul's. Also, the dog was sick due to my driving.

The cost of running a van made it more urgent than ever that we gain charitable status. This was not my forte, and we needed someone who was good at official paperwork and administration. Once again, God's timing was spot on! We had a team of around twenty volunteers, all female, to staff the drop-in and outreach, but now a new volunteer joined us. Helen Hill was a lawyer, praise God, and we eagerly approached her for help in forming a constitution and with all the legalities involved in applying for charitable status and forming a company limited by guarantee. Helen successfully took on the task and One25 became a registered charity, enabling us to apply for funding.

This was an important and huge step forward, and was part of my vision for being a successful, professional organization which could look after its volunteers and oversee the work effectively.

From the very beginning it was decided that as part of our constitution we should be founded and work on Christian principles. Not everyone who worked with One25 was a Christian – indeed, just three out of the four of our original vision group were Christian. I had always wanted the organization to be open to volunteers of any faith or belief, and also to ex-working women. But I felt strongly – and so did others – that Jesus was the reason I was there and had started the work. And although people can change and heal by themselves, I was more and more convinced that true restoration only came through the loving power of God. We worded our constitution carefully, making clear that we were never going to be exclusive about faith, but that anyone who worked with us did need to understand and respect our founding values. It means a lot to me that this faith-based and inclusive approach is still the basis of One25's work today.

The gift of the van transformed the project. We were able to drive much further than I had been able to walk on my evening outreach. We initially went out just one night each week with hot water in flasks to make tea or coffee, and homemade cake and chocolate bars. We also had condoms and cigarettes – provided by Cliff and Dorothy respectively! A decision was taken by the management team that for reasons of safety we should go in teams of three. This would include a driver, who would always stay in the driver's seat, and two workers, who would operate from the back of the van with the women. One of the three would be nominated the team leader.

Hot drinks and food would be offered, either for the women to eat in the van or take away with them. The main object, though, was to engage the women in conversation and to earn their trust. Team leaders were encouraged to start each evening session with prayer. This took place in a small room in the One25 building, where we also kept our stocks and equipment. If individual volunteers were uncomfortable with prayer, that was no problem – they would just sit quietly during the prayer time and listen. We also began the habit of debriefing at the end of sessions, which was especially important if there had been any stresses, or difficult situations.

On the first night we went out, we met six different women, none of whom knew who we were or what we were about. However, they enjoyed coming into the safety and warmth of the van, and enjoyed the coffee and chocolate cake. Initially our outreach was only into St Paul's, but this was later extended to include Montpelier and Easton – two nearby neighbourhoods. We extended the van outreach to three nights each week and word quickly spread among the women that we would be coming.

Many more women made contact with us through the van than ever did in the drop-in. It became clear that many had no safe accommodation of their own. Some were sleeping on sofas in 'friends'' homes, and others were with boyfriends/ pimps who controlled their lives. Most of them had a drug habit and many were hungry. Their lives were chaotic, and the van was an accessible and meaningful way forward for working with them.

In no time at all, the van outreach was extended to a further two nights each week, so we were now available from Monday to Friday between 8 p.m. and midnight. In addition to the drinks, homemade cake and chocolate bars, we added two varieties of sandwiches and some fruit. These were gratefully received, particularly during that first winter of 1997, which was bitterly cold. Conditions inside the van were not ideal as we were unable to stand upright because of the low ceiling. Also, getting into the back of the van through the rear doors posed a problem for the women, who sometimes were wearing tight skirts and high-heeled shoes, making the step up into the van difficult. We purchased a small step to overcome that problem and offer dignity for the women coming inside. Always the need for flexibility!

It was so exciting how quickly the van became loved by the women, and we soon discovered, to our amusement, that they referred to it as 'The Custard Tart'! It was, after all, bright yellow. We would regularly see a minimum of fifteen women in one evening, and often many more.

Winter 1997 saw our first Christmas on the van. Dorothy's husband, Ronald, a retired professor from the University of Bristol, decorated the van with Christmas lights, which delighted the women. Also, a very generous volunteer in the project gave me £50 and asked me to spend it on a gift for each woman.

I had a good relationship with a florist in St Paul's. Sally had often in the past given flowers at very low prices to me and to friends of deceased homeless people for funeral services. Once again, I approached Sally and asked whether she could help. I had in my mind that I would like pink roses. On Christmas Eve morning, I called at Sally's florist shop. To my absolute delight, Sally had fifty beautiful single pink roses, each in a small phial of water, and charged us just £1 each.

That night, we went out on the van outreach with the roses and some Christmas cards. Our first stop was for just one woman. She was visibly unhappy as she stepped onto the van and seemed full of pent-up anger. I remember that she was quiet as she had a hot drink and some food and did not want to engage in conversation. The time came for her to leave the van and it was at this point that I gave her the rose and a card.

Immediately, out came the anger. She shouted at me, 'What the **** do you think you're doing?' and called me names. She demanded to know what we wanted from her – 'After all,' she snapped, 'nobody gives someone a gift without wanting something in return.'

I explained as best I could that we just wanted to give her a gift at Christmas to show that we valued her as a woman, and that we wanted nothing in return. She hesitated for quite a few moments, close up to me, studying my expression. Then her face melted into a smile, as she said that this would be the only gift, and the only card, she would receive at Christmas. She left the van with the pink rose in her hand.

By the end of that Christmas Eve outreach, those of us volunteers on the van were deeply affected by the sight of the women standing on the streets, each holding a pink rose in their hands. We also wondered just what the punters might think, as they approached each special woman.

10

Godsends

Five nights a week between 8 p.m. and midnight, our bright yellow Ford Transit van could be seen driving slowly around particular streets in Bristol, with three women in the front, their eyes peeled, constantly surveying the scene. For more than a hundred women working on the streets, the yellow van with its supply of coffee, food and condoms became a familiar part of their lives.

Sometimes the mood in the van was sombre; the women sharing their distress and weariness at surviving a life of drugs, violence and abuse. All too often, a woman had been the subject of a brutal attack or rape and was too afraid to report it to the police. On other occasions, they would spend time just chatting and also wanting to know about our lives – our children, families, homes. I think they liked knowing that not all women lived like they did. Relationships of trust were built up. After all, we were all just women sharing something of our lives and ourselves with each other.

It became clear to me in the early days of setting up One25 that gaining credibility with other agencies was going to be essential. This was the case with statutory agencies such as the NHS, Social Services and the police, and other voluntary agencies working with people abusing drugs and alcohol. Money is always tight in the voluntary sector and it quickly became evident that not everyone welcomed One25 as an agency wanting to work alongside others. In some cases, we were seen as Christian do-gooders who wouldn't last, and in others as competitors for available money and services. Still others felt we were stereotyping the women as 'victims' and should back off.

It took determination and a strong professional approach to show that we were there for the long haul and were committed to making a difference for good in our city and in the lives of the women we valued. It's testament to our tenaciousness as well as our commitment to doing things well that One25 is a strong and well-respected organization today.

Individual contacts with statutory agencies were not always brilliant. I remember going with one of the women we were working with to a consultant at the Bristol Royal Infirmary. Dominique had been referred to this specialist because her hair was falling out. The consultant looked very official, sitting up ramrod straight behind his desk.

Dominique said to him, 'My hair's come out. I used to have beautiful hair, and it's all coming out.'

The man said, 'Well, if you will smoke crack, that's what you have to expect.'

In a flash, she was up and over the desk, she had hold of him by the tie. She was calling him an effing idiot, and he was saying, 'Get her off me! Get her off me!'

I managed to get her off him. 'Come on, Dominique,' I said. 'This man just doesn't understand the issues. Let's go.' As she let go of him, the consultant opened a drawer of his desk, took out a wig, skidded it over the desk towards us and said, 'Have this,' and off we went.

Thankfully not all interactions went like this – although if people are not trained to understand the complex lives and backgrounds of the women we work with, how can they be expected to respond appropriately? Another woman we worked with, Yasmin, had a brilliant relationship with her psychiatrist. She was from a tough background. Her alcoholic father had left the family long ago. Her mother had been on LSD most of her life, and was not really available or even aware much of the time.

I remember the first time I saw this psychiatrist. He was handsome and dapper, terribly smart and a bit flamboyant with a quirky bow tie. I thought, 'Gosh, she's going to hate him,' but he actually built a brilliant relationship with Yasmin. She calls him 'Dr F' because she can't say his surname, and he calls her 'Yaz' and always asks how her daughter is. Together, they manage her medication so she has the best chance of being able to operate safely and constructively in the world.

We developed particularly positive working relationships with the specialist Vice team who oversaw much of the policing in St Paul's. They were caring and professional people who understood their job and its impact on the women working there. Within months of starting the van outreach, we began to notify them every night when we were leaving – giving them the names of each volunteer on the van – and then contacting them again to let them know we had arrived back safely. We began to trust them, and they us, and there would be instances when we would share information and work together for the benefit of vulnerable people.

A number of times in my working life, the Vice team contacted me asking if I'd seen a particular woman recently, because she had slipped off their radar. They weren't keeping tabs, or wanting to arrest her. Generally, it was to check that there hadn't been another murder.

Although we were using the One25 building for van preparation, and for keeping our flasks, snacks and other equipment in, we still didn't have an office. At Easter in 1997, I had approached Bristol Christian Fellowship to ask if I could have the use of a room in their building. This unused church building was situated on Grosvenor Road, St Paul's, right in the heart of the working area for the female sex workers. My request went to the fellowship's trustees, who asked how much rent we could pay. I had a boldness and a confidence which I think came from knowing we were doing God's work, in God's way. So I replied, '£1 a month' and, wonderfully, they agreed.

I moved into the Grosvenor Centre later that year and had the use of an upstairs room as an office, together with the telephone. I was now able to have a base as the One25 manager, and to establish the project on a more professional footing. I remained committed to consolidating the work as a professional outfit, where all volunteers were well supported and there was the best chance of us continuing, growing and becoming sustainable.

I remember being so delighted with having an office, and yet every positive step left me hungry for more. Over the years I had had a number of meetings with consultants in the sexual health clinic of the Bristol Royal Infirmary, concerning the necessity for sex workers to have open access to healthcare, rather than needing to make and attend appointments. I already knew from the Candle Project that for men and women leading chaotic lives due to drug and/or alcohol abuse, keeping appointments is just not possible. I sat in my office, right in the middle of St Paul's, grateful but still dreaming. One day, I resolved, One25 would have its very own drop-in centre here too, and at that point, we would have a weekly medical clinic on-site – offering help exactly where the need was – where people could get to it.

In the meantime, we had some rather more immediate issues – not least, the ongoing cost of running the van. Early in the new year of 1998, Sister Mary told me that a Catholic order of nuns was moving to a smaller building and that they had sold their large property. Mary was under the impression that there might just be some 'spare' money to be put to a good use. She suggested that we should write to this order, putting the case for funding our van. As a result of our letter, a senior male member of their administrative team agreed to visit us and look at the van, giving Mary and me the opportunity to explain how our project worked.

At this point, we kept the van overnight in a tight, gated parking space off a narrow lane in St Paul's, behind the Grosvenor Centre. So, on the day our visitor was coming, we moved the van out of its parking space and parked it on the street so that we had space to walk around it, and open the doors. We invited the man inside the van, and sat in the back, explaining our work with the back doors ajar.

You can imagine what happened next! As we were discussing how the outreach worked, there was a tap on the back door and one of the female sex workers peered in. She asked what we were doing there during the day, and could she please have something to eat. Well, no amount of explaining could have demonstrated the importance of our work as well as this woman did. Her arrival clinched it for us, and we were awarded £1,000 a year for three years, to keep the van on the road. It was another example of God's perfect timing!

Once I had my office space in the Grosvenor Centre, it didn't take long for the women to notice, and soon I would find a few of them waiting outside when I arrived at work at 8.30 in the morning. I began inviting them in for a hot drink and toast and this, quite naturally, began to extend throughout the whole day.

This was not particularly safe, as I was working alone. However, not long after my move, a lady approached me to ask if we could talk about the possibility of her becoming a volunteer. That lady was Pat Dimond. Pat had retired the previous year and had heard about One25. She was unsure about her suitability as a volunteer but nevertheless felt prompted by God to approach us.

Early in 1998 Pat agreed to come to the Grosvenor Centre every Tuesday to help me with administration, and this quickly developed as Pat met the women who called in during the day. Pat asked me to take her on foot outreach around St Paul's, and we started doing this on Tuesday afternoons. It became something we both looked forward to, talking together and often praying, as we walked the streets of our neighbourhood.

Pat was literally a Godsend to me and to One25. She was loved by the women and the staff. I so looked forward to Tuesdays, and Pat's company and help. This gentle woman had begun by underestimating her capacity, but trusting in God's calling, and she ended up being our longest-serving volunteer. She had such a generosity of spirit and I learned much from her.

We were also joined in the management team by a very wise local lady, Carol Self. Carol was the wife of the local vicar of St Agnes Church in St Paul's and brought sound common sense and a knowledge of the local area to our team, together with a great deal of compassion.

It was becoming clear, though, that I needed someone to work alongside me in the Grosvenor Centre whenever I was there, not just on Tuesdays, for safety reasons.

This culminated late one afternoon when I was alone in the centre. It was winter, and I was getting ready to go home, around 5 p.m. The team that day had been working on the van with underage twin girls and we were extremely concerned about their welfare. The police and Social Services had been informed of our contact with these very vulnerable girls, and were involved. The doorbell rang. The front door had two small windows in it, and I could see the face of one of these underage girls. She was banging on the door and pleading with me to let her in.

As I was opening the door to her, a man pushed her out of the way and burst into the Grosvenor Centre. This was the man I knew to be pimping these young teenage sisters and he was angry that One25 was working to have them removed into safety. He started shouting at me and pushing me around the room, saying he knew I was alone in the building.

I remember that I reacted calmly – and this is not like me at all, I was very frightened. I told him that I was not alone, but that there were three others present with me. He clearly didn't believe this at first, but I insisted, and said they would come to my help. With that, he turned on his heel and started walking to the front door, shouting that I had to come out of the building sooner or later and he would be waiting. It was absolutely true that I had three others with me. I had, of course, been referring to God the Father, God the Son and God the Holy Spirit.

As soon as I had shut the front door I could hear the telephone ringing in my office, which was upstairs. I ran up the stairs and picked up the telephone. It was the vice liaison officer from Avon and Somerset Police. She immediately picked up from my voice that I was a bit shaky and I told her what had happened. She offered to send a car over to make sure I was safe leaving the building.

The pimp who had confronted me was frightening, and a well-known dangerous character in the area, but I politely refused the offer of a police car, thanking the vice officer nonetheless. I was afraid, but I knew that if I showed that fear, I would be finished – I would literally not be able to do my work in St Paul's any more. By this time, everybody knew who I was. In a strange way, I was accepted – even though I was working to help free people from the hold of drugs and prostitution, which were the backbone of the local economy. Even the dealers would give a tiny nod as I passed – there was a kind of acknowledgement, a respect for where I fitted in.

I was not being foolhardy in refusing the police car. I knew that the women would not come to One25 if I did not have credibility in the neighbourhood. Pimps, partners, boyfriends, all had to know that One25, and I personally, were not to be messed with. I'd earned my place there. If I'd had a police car waiting outside – if I was someone who called in the statutory law-enforcers and needed their back-up when things got scary – it would have finished me.

I'm not ashamed to say that I was trembling when I left the office, shortly after the conversation with the vice liaison officer, but wonderfully, there was no sign of the pimp. I'm not sure I see this episode as showing any courage – it's just something I knew I had to do. I was still the woman who had been scared and nervous of the homeless people I saw when going into the Salvation Army for church services some years ago. What a work God had done in me. Whatever courage I did have came from him.

And God sometimes used unconventional ways of keeping me safe.

Next door to the Grosvenor Centre was a taxi company, which had a large window onto the street, and a number of men always stationed at the front desk or sitting around it, chatting and answering the telephone. They never missed a thing, and I was pretty sure that they would have heard the shouting that time from the pimp and the young girl at my door. It's not that they would have come out to rescue me if I'd been physically attacked, necessarily, but I do think that the pimp who had threatened me would have been aware of their presence and their eyes on him.

The taxi people did come to my aid one time when I was waiting outside the Grosvenor Centre to meet a new volunteer. I had my rucksack on, and it was probably 8 p.m. or so in the evening. A Somali man came down the road. He had quat (a chewable hallucinogenic) sticking out of his mouth. He was off his head. He came right up to me and was propositioning me. Silly man! He was way beyond distinguishing between a street-based sex worker and a middle-aged project manager!

I was saying to him, 'Leave me alone, go away,' but I didn't feel I could leave or run away, because I was waiting for this new volunteer, and I didn't want her arriving and being there alone without me. He became more and more insistent, and

I was just beginning to think, 'I'll have to leave,' when one of the Jamaicans from the taxi company came out of his office. He just went up to this guy and said, 'Move on.' The guy left me alone, and the taxi man went back inside.

This potential protection also proved to be a good thing when Cliff and I changed our car for a smarter, though still second-hand, model. I popped into the cab company, and asked them to keep an eye on our new car while I was out on night outreach once. They nodded sagely and replied, 'There ain't no **** that happens on Grosvenor Road that we don't know about.' That car never had a scratch on it.

Shortly after that incident of being alone with the aggressive pimp, I was invited to speak at a local ladies' luncheon group in Redland Parish Church Hall – in a fairly affluent area of Bristol (my life was full of contrasting scenarios!). After a very pleasant lunch and my talk, I was approached by two Christian ladies, who were from a parish church in Bath. One of them, Chris White, said she was interested in volunteering with One25. We clicked straight away, and after volunteering for a short time on the van, Chris agreed to also join me in the office three days each week – unpaid. This was an enormous answer to prayer, and once again transformative for the project.

Chris quickly took on responsibility and related very well to the women. I remain profoundly grateful for Chris's friendship and her willingness to give of herself without financial remuneration. Chris is a strong, compassionate, courageous woman of faith and I thank God for her. She was a joy to work with. We were both risk-takers and pioneers, who loved getting things done, but also needed our backs watched! More than once, Chris and I would get each other out of potentially sticky situations.

Because Chris was a member of an Anglican church, when she became a part of the One25 staff we were able to apply to the Church Urban Fund for financing. They sent along a representative to interview Chris and myself, and to view the van. This resulted in a grant of £9,000 for the project, split over three years, to be used as we saw fit. It was decided by the management team that this funding should be used to pay Chris and me for the work we did. It was split between the two of us, giving each of us the princely sum of £1,500 a year for the next three years.

It was the first salary One25 ever paid, and it was worth so much more than the money. It was a sign from God that he was with me – confirmation that I was doing a valuable and valued work, which was well-regarded, properly supported and recognized. It was my first income for two and a half years.

11

Squeezing in a Prayer

However much God was blessing our work, and however many people respected what we were doing, the van outreach was not universally well received. In one of the localities where the women worked, there was significant opposition to the van, and a number of complaints. We arranged a meeting with the police and local residents. In this meeting it transpired that the residents thought that the van was encouraging women to work in their neighbourhood. We explained that this was not the case and that in fact, when we could, we encouraged women not to work close to residential homes or near schools. Nevertheless, a local vigilante group formed.

One night, while we were parked up and the women were enjoying a hot drink, the van started rocking from side to side. This was alarming, and potentially very dangerous. A small group of young men had formed around the van in the darkness and were trying to push us over. Thankfully, Chris White was the team leader, in the driver's seat, and she quickly started the engine. With one young man still on the running board, she drove the van down the road, zigzagging as she went. He jumped off, and we made a safe escape. But for Chris's quick thinking and action, the outcome could have been extremely serious. The following morning, we checked in with the police and reported the incident.

There are many stories involving the van outreach, from the inspiring to the comical to the frankly perplexing! Safety on the van was always a primary consideration, and we were all serious about keeping to policies and practices, but things could still go quite easily wrong. I remember one hot summer evening when everyone was feeling relaxed. We were parked up on Fishponds Road, one of the busy working areas for the women. Earlier in the day, I had received a telephone call from the vice liaison officer warning us that there was a man, Q, newly arrived in the city, who was known to be violent and dangerous. She warned us to have nothing to do with him.

This is where I made a big mistake as team leader and van driver, and as someone who should have known much better. As I have said, it was a hot night, and my first mistake was to have the window open alongside me in the driver's seat. My second mistake was to have my back to the window as I joined in the chatter with the volunteers and women in the rear of the van. Everything was going well until a man thrust his head through my open window demanding coffee, sandwiches and condoms. It was Q.

I tried to take calm control of the situation, and quietly refused his demand, telling him that this was a women-only service and advising him to remove his head. He refused and I continued asking him to do so. He was not particularly unpleasant, but he just kept demanding coffee, food and condoms. And this is where I made my final mistake. I told him that I was going to start the engine of the van and would move off, and that he should remove himself now while he had the chance.

He did not do so, and I had no choice but to keep my word. I started the engine and slowly moved down the road, still with

Q's head in the window. I kept asking him to remove his head but he kept moving with us.

Not quite knowing what to do, but not wanting to go back on what I'd said, I increased speed slightly and wound up the window a bit – which was stupid because, of course, that made it more difficult for him to get his head out, rather than easier. By this time, he was running alongside the van, and I came to my senses, realizing how dangerous this had become. I slowed down, came to a halt, and wound down the window. Q removed his head and walked away.

I knew I had behaved foolishly, putting this man's life at risk. We drove away from the area very relieved that nothing bad had happened. The women on the van confirmed that this was indeed the man the police had referred to. He had approached a number of them and threatened violence unless they gave him money or drugs.

An hour or so later, as we once again drove up Fishponds Road and stopped for women to come on the van, Q appeared again, at my now closed window. I shouted through the window, asking him what he wanted, reiterating that this was a service for women only. Q then produced our small plastic step, which we had left behind when I drove away from our encounter earlier in the evening. He was smiling, and pleased to be returning our property to us!

The following morning, I reported my actions to the police vice liaison officer and to our management team. Carol Self, then chair of the management team, reprimanded me for my actions, quite rightly so.

A further and somewhat baffling result of my encounter with Q was that on several occasions following that evening, and particularly when he saw me on foot, he would act as a friend, smiling at me and raising his hand for a 'high five'. I really didn't want or need that kind of interaction – not from a violent man who was attempting to extort money and sex from the women I cared about. I certainly didn't want to be seen being apparently friendly with such a threatening character.

Whether he thought I had let him off lightly, or just had no sense of what genuine friendship was, I don't know. Things are rarely cut and dried. Thankfully, he was only around for a few weeks before disappearing from St Paul's again, leaving me mightily relieved.

The van outreach was often the time and place where women had the opportunity to really open up about their lives, and for us to listen and come alongside them. Often this was at times of pain such as violence or rape, but other times these opportunities came seemingly out of nowhere. One such summer evening we were parked up with just a few women on the van. One of our 'regulars' arrived on the pillion seat of a motorbike. She was clothed entirely in red PVC. Normally Connie was very bubbly and talkative but on this occasion she just sat quietly and enjoyed a drink and a sandwich.

The other women left the van, leaving Connie alone with us. At that point I asked her if there was anything we could do to help as she appeared not to be herself. She replied that there was nothing we could do. After a short while I spoke to her again, offering to listen if there was something she wanted to share, or possibly help with a practical problem. Again, Connie replied that we could not help her. At this point, I asked her instead if she would allow me to pray with her, acknowledging that maybe we were not in a position to help her. Connie agreed to this.

We were sitting opposite each other on the long side seats of the van. I asked her if I could touch her arm as we prayed, and she agreed. I leaned across the van, placing my hand on her arm and started to pray. Immediately she protested. 'What are you on?' she exclaimed. 'Everyone knows that when you pray you get down on your knees and put your hands together!' Surprised, I quickly apologized and together we knelt in the van, hands together. I prayed a simple prayer. It was surreal, in the immediacy of the van and the neighbourhood – Connie in her red PVC and me in jeans and a shirt, praying together on our knees in the very narrow space between the bench seats.

After I prayed, Connie broke down in tears, saying no one had ever prayed with her in her life before. Then she opened up and shared something of her very serious problems. Connie was in debt to a drug dealer. There was no way she could pay, and she needed to leave Bristol, quickly. Chris and I arranged to meet her the following day at her flat.

At the flat, we helped Connie gather together some clothes and a few possessions, hastily pushing them into plastic bags. We were just about ready to leave when there was loud knocking on her door. She peered through a small window and spotted the drug dealer she owed money to.

My car was parked outside in the road to the side of the front door and we decided upon an emergency escape plan. I went first, climbing out of a side window onto the lawn and crawling across to the car, hoping that the dealer would not see me. Thankfully, he was intent upon banging on the front door, and so missed me. As soon as I reached the car, I signalled to Chris and Connie and they also climbed out of the window and ran to the car, where I had the engine running. The dealer saw what was happening then, and chased after us, but we were clear and sped down the road and away to safety. It was definitely one of my most scary moments. We drove her to the bus station and purchased a ticket on a bus to another city, where Connie had a relative she could stay with.

Connie left Bristol for several years and during that time, she succeeded in coming off drugs and leaving sex work. That was a wonderful answer to prayer. I know God met Connie and me when we knelt, cramped and constricted in the van, to make a simple request for his help.

Another scary moment came one dark evening, when I was the team leader on the van. As usual we were a team of three, and for one volunteer it was her first time out on the van for several years following a period of illness. The third person was a new member of staff who had only started working with One25 the previous day. We prepared well before leaving the safety of the parking place in Franklyn Lane, St Paul's, and were each confident of our roles. I was the driver and reversed out into Franklyn Lane, which is very narrow with just enough space for one large vehicle such as the van.

I had the two volunteers alongside me in the front seat, and was about to drive forward onto Grosvenor Road when I heard a lot of shouting, and saw men jumping from windows and over the back walls of the property next to One25. These men were followed, out of the windows and over the walls, by armed police. We had reversed straight into a police stakeout!

The police officers had huge guns, and were shouting at us, 'Get down! Get down!' – which I, for one, couldn't do, because the steering wheel was in the way! I shouted to my two other crew members to get down. The police then shouted, 'Move back! Move back!' I put the van into reverse and started moving rapidly backwards down the tiny lane. As I did so, about five Somali men with machetes surrounded the van. They were running to get away from the police, and it was so narrow in the lane that I could hear them banging against the sides of the van as they squeezed past.

They were immediately pursued by police officers, who yelled at me again to 'Move!' which I did! I have never before, or since, reversed at such a speed, in the dark, with the fear of squashing people between the van and the walls on either side of a narrow lane, in order to get away.

We reached the bottom of the lane into Franklyn Street, and managed to turn onto St Nicholas' Road. I drove a little way down this street and stopped at a safe place. The machete men and the police had disappeared, and we could no longer hear them. We stopped and debriefed on what had happened. What an intense experience for us all – and especially for my two crew members. For one of them, this was her first-ever experience of volunteering with One25, for the other it was the first experience back with us after some years!

Thankfully, both women decided they still wanted to continue the evening's outreach, but not until we had all opened up the flasks and enjoyed a cup of restorative tea together.

The van was also invaluable for helping women to move house when they were allocated flats or, more importantly, in emergency cases of domestic abuse. Susan had a small house in St Paul's for herself and her son. However, she was being pimped by a violent and coercive man who made life very unpleasant for her.

One afternoon we received a telephone call from her at the Burns Unit in Frenchay Hospital. Her 'boyfriend' had poured boiling water over her as she lay in bed, because she felt too unwell to go out to work on the streets. She had dialled 999 for an ambulance and Social Services sent an emergency social worker to take care of Susan's son.

Susan spent a number of weeks in hospital recovering from her burns, during which time she contacted Bristol City Council to ask for a transfer away from St Paul's due to the domestic abuse. The housing people were brilliant and responded swiftly. When she was discharged from hospital, I met with her to discuss the next step in her recovery, as she had been put on a methadone prescription in hospital due to her heroin addiction.

Susan was allocated a two-bedroom house in another area of Bristol and asked us to move her furniture and belongings, which I agreed to do. I asked Chris and Dorothy Milne for their help and advised them to wear boots because of the risk of needles on the floors of the house which Susan was leaving. Also, Susan had several dogs and from past experience I expected the house to be messy. We loaded the furniture onto the van and drove to the new house.

For Susan this was the beginning of recovery in every sense. She and her son loved their new home and took a pride in keeping it safe and clean. Because she was no longer dependent on illegal drugs, Susan was able to really take hold of her life. She stopped sex working and concentrated on building a new life. She is still living in her 'new' home some seventeen or so years later, has a full-time job and is no longer supported by benefits. She has become a lovely friend to me. Susan is a strong woman and is now back in touch with her family and accepted by them.

Sadly, Susan did not feel able to take action against her former partner, due to her fear of him. He moved on to another vulnerable woman, who also experienced violence and abuse.

The van was a wonderful resource, but with women queueing for toast every morning when I arrived for work at the

Grosvenor Centre, it had also become clear that we needed a drop-in centre, not just an upstairs office.

Once again, I approached the trustees of Bristol Christian Fellowship, our landlords. I requested the use of the whole building at an increased rent of £200 per month – the amount the management team had agreed to allocate. This would allow us to develop the whole of the ground floor hall as a large sitting room and use the existing kitchen for food preparation and drinks. They agreed, praise God! This ongoing support and generosity from Bristol Christian Fellowship allowed the project to move forward into the next phase.

We secured funding to carpet the floor and furnish the room with IKEA sofas and small tables. There were two toilets on the ground floor, and we converted a back store room into a shower and laundry room. This was much appreciated when we opened in 1998. At last the women could come into the drop-in four afternoons each week for a cooked meal. They could shower, wash their clothes and engage with the staff and volunteers.

We purchased a number of large storage boxes, and labelled them, so that each woman could safely store her belongings. Many of the women were essentially homeless, and spent their days or nights sleeping on other people's floors, in squats, shelters or wherever they could find a place. How do you keep things that are precious to you in that situation? Years later, I can still see in my mind that row of named boxes, and the precious, personal things inside. These often included photographs of children who had been removed into care. Sometimes there were pictures of their parents, or other family members, together with items of clothing.

This was a safe, women-only space and often our service users would come in to eat and sleep in safety, although it was not possible for them to stay overnight under any circumstances. Notices were placed around the ground floor area clearly stating that drug or alcohol use would not be tolerated on the premises and would lead to being banned from the project.

I rarely had to use the threat of banning someone, but it was important to have these policies, and know we would follow through on them if we needed to. This was especially true one Christmas, when I was knocked out by one of the women.

Elsie had been to the drop-in during the day on Christmas Eve – we were open till 5 p.m. She wouldn't do her washing, for some reason. I kept saying, 'Do your washing, Elsie, because we need to close soon, and we'll be closed for a few days,' but she didn't, and in the end, she left the washing behind when she went. I knew it would be a huge mistake.

We all went home and later that evening, I was out on the van – it was Christmas morning by now, probably 1 a.m. or so. We were actually on Grosvenor Road, which was the worst place Elsie could have seen me. She came running over, saying, 'I wanna do my washing!'

I said, 'No, I'm not opening up.'

Elsie was not happy about this, and told me so! All the cab drivers came out to have a look at the argument. I stood my ground. I thought, 'If I let her in now, we'll never get her out again. She won't do the washing, she'll want to sleep on the sofa, and we all need to go home.'

'I've said it's not open, Elsie,' I repeated. 'I'm not opening up.'

That's when she threw a massive punch, and it knocked me out.

When I came round, on the pavement, Elsie had disappeared. The volunteers helped me pick myself up and checked me over. Thankfully I had no lasting injuries.

When we reopened after Christmas, I typed a letter banning her from the drop-in centre and the van until we met to discuss her behaviour because of the physical violence.

She stayed away for a whole year – until the next Christmas Eve, in fact. I was just about to leave the centre and at 5 p.m., she turned up at the door.

'Here we go,' I thought.

'I've come to say I'm sorry,' said Elsie. 'Can I come back?'

I believed her. 'Yes, come back,' I said. 'I'm only sorry that it's taken a whole year.' We hugged. We were reconciled. She started using the service again.

Sometime later, I supported her in court, and eventually helped her to leave Bristol, to a place the Probation Service had found for her, in another city. In the court, you'd have laughed your head off. She had been violent before, and this offence was similar. She knew there was a chance she would get a prison sentence. However, they decided to give her a probation order.

When the three magistrates announced her sentence, she was over the moon. They told her, 'This is your very last chance. We believe you want to change.' All of a sudden, Elsie leapt out of the defendant's box, ran up to where I was sitting, and pulled something out of her bag. It was a box of chocolates!

She ran with the box of chocolates up to the magistrates' bench, and presented it to them. She was actually bowing and saying, 'Thank you, m'Lord! Thank you, m'Lady!' They laughed. We all laughed. She knew in a way that she was

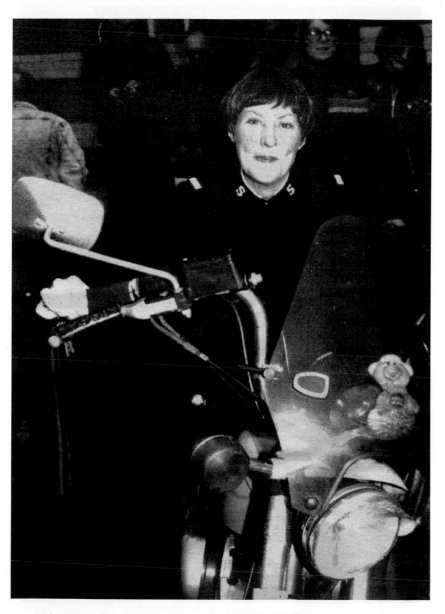

Val on a Harley-Davidson motorcycle (courtesy of the Salvation Army)

Original founding group, left to right: Sr Mary Donnelly, Dr Dorothy Milne, Sr Annaliese, Val Jeal

Away day on the Black Mountains; left to right: Helen Hill, Brigid Morgan (nee Dolan), Chris White, Val

Val taking possession of the gift of a van from Cornerstone Ministries

Inside of the first outreach van 'the Custard Tart'

Craft session in the drop-in

One25 Grosvenor Centre drop-in sitting room

Chris White at a One25 Christmas party

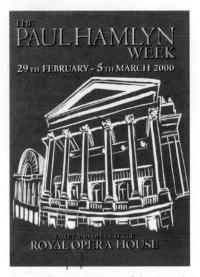

Royal Opera House flyer (courtesy of the Royal Opera House)

Day out on the Quantock Hills with residents from The Well

Franklyn Lane, site of police/criminal gang encounter
(courtesy of Jude Simpson)

Naomi House lounge

Naomi House resident's bedroom

putting on a performance, but she was also completely serious. She was so grateful that she had been given that chance. She wouldn't have known at that moment whether she would have the strength to change, to see it through, but she knew that someone had given her a chance. And that made all the difference.

Elsie is now living independently, back in Bristol. She spent some time away, and that helped her sort herself out. She now has her own flat, and she looks after her dog. She's on methadone rather than heroin, she's not working, and she hasn't reoffended. She took the chance, and made the change.

One of One25's supporters donated a television for us to have at the Grosvenor Centre drop-in, but we did not have a licence for programmes, as we felt there would just be too many arguments over choosing the channel. Instead, we had a video recorder, and were able to show films. Two firm favourites were *Pretty Woman* and *Titanic*.

One afternoon while the women were watching a film, there was a minor disturbance taking the attention of Chris, myself and the volunteer on duty with us. As we were sorting out the problem, we spotted one of the women moving quickly towards the outside door, clutching something under her arm. We also noticed that the room had gone quiet – including the film.

The woman, Carol, ran down Grosvenor Road with Chris and me in hot pursuit. She reached the Black and White Café and ducked inside just before we caught up with her. Chris and I stopped at the door, considering what action we should take. Before we could decide, the door opened and Carol appeared, with our video recorder. Behind her, in the café we heard a voice admonishing, 'Have respect, give it back!'

What a result!

It might seem odd to some people that characters like those in the Black and White Café, who were deeply involved in the criminal underworld, still had a sense of morality – still felt it was wrong to steal a video recorder from One25. But I've seen many examples of people having strong personal moral codes, even while living a life which many others would consider immoral.

Most of the women working on the streets, for example, felt they were considerably more upright than a thief, because they were not taking anything that belonged to someone else. The only people they were doing harm to was themselves – they were not hurting another person.

How wonderful, then, to meet a God who cares that you're hurting yourself, who values you and who wants you to be whole.

Some years ago, I accompanied Tasha, one of the female sex workers, to purchase yet another Bible. I had probably already given her two, which had been lost or damaged. On this occasion, we drove to Wesley Owen, a Christian bookshop, and she selected a Bible with large print.

The shop was busy with people browsing books and cards. As we approached the desk for me to pay for the Bible she had chosen, Tasha held it high in the air and in a very loud voice declared, 'See this Bible, everyone? It says in here that prostitutes will go to heaven before all you lot!' She paused for a moment, for dramatic effect, then declared triumphantly, 'And *I'm* a prostitute!'

A silence fell over the shop. I felt myself go a delicate shade of red. The lady at the till looked more than a little surprised. But Tasha seems to have read Matthew 21:31, in which Jesus, in the Parable of the Two Sons, tells the people, 'the tax collectors and the prostitutes are entering the kingdom of God ahead of you.'

A woman despised and rejected by many had read the Bible and found a God who accepted her into his kingdom. Hallelujah!

12

From Abuse to Trust, from Beach to Ballet

We now had a safe drop-in service which was on the working patch for the women. It was accessible, welcoming, and was used by them. This seemed the time to once again approach the NHS Sexual Health Clinic concerning on-site health support. The management team and I were clear that any possible support needed to be both diagnostic and treatment – all in one session and in the Grosvenor Centre. Agreement was reached for a weekly NHS clinic with a doctor and a nurse each Tuesday afternoon in a dedicated room in the drop-in. This was a huge step forward and much appreciated by our client group.

The drop-in was valuable in providing a safe place for women to engage with staff and volunteers on a one-to-one basis. Their complex lives brought up many issues which could not have been openly discussed on the van and which now could begin to be addressed. It was also the environment in which women could start believing that they may have choices in their lives. Again, something that could only be considered in a place of safety and confidentiality.

Other activities were added to the drop-in, such as jewellery making. Each week Maureen, a local artist, brought her materials to the centre and made rings and other jewellery with the women. Another favourite activity was making cards to send to their families. Several of the regular drop-in users started writing amazing poetry. This was often heart-rending and an outlet for their emotions and past experiences.

Linda was not a regular drop-in user, as her life was particularly chaotic and violent. We mostly had contact with her through the van outreach. Linda had been using heroin from the age of 15, having been introduced to drugs and injected by her 'uncle'. Linda's life was in shreds. Her three children had been taken into care and her drug habit was out of control. When Linda did come to the drop-in, she sometimes wrote poetry which reflected the horrors of her life, yet also showed an extraordinary capacity for courage and hope.

At one point, when Linda came to the drop-in, she was preparing to go to a safe house which had opened in the Midlands run by some Catholic nuns. She wrote a poem about this potential turning point in her life, and asked us to publish it in the One25 newsletter.

Change the Cycle (a poem by Linda)

I'm doing something strange.
I'm doing something new
Changing my life, taking control of my life
The life I long to be whole.

I've crawled in the gutter
I've sold all I have
I've lost all my friends through overdoses and diseases.

But I'm starting afresh, I'm starting anew.
And if I can make amends, I'll make it up to you.
But even if forgiveness is something I don't receive,
From the people I've betrayed,
I can understand if you don't think I've paid.

But remember this, I'm doing this to live
I'm doing this for me.
Because unless I change, death is the only thing left.

There are a hundred reasons to change
But only one that will work.
Because I want to, I need to, it's got to be for me.

For any other reason it's back on drugs for me.
And then a pine box, in a hole, in a nameless grave.

It's my life – I've got to give it a try.
There are a million hurting voices crying out in pain
They are saying seize the chance, make the change
Life can be fun, you can make it work
Change the cycle, start with rebirth.

In this poem Linda showed incredible insight into her life, and a sober understanding of where her life would end up, unless she was able to change.

On the last occasion I saw Linda before she left Bristol, she was approaching the van to say goodbye to us. I was in the driver's seat and Linda was in the road. A young man on a bicycle rode towards her in a menacing way, shouting abuse.

Linda turned around and he ripped from her neck the gold locket she was wearing, and rode away.

Linda was distraught – the locket contained the photograph of her small child who had recently been removed into care. How cruel. She was angry and crushed, and we were at a loss as to how we could possibly comfort her.

Linda was a courageous and intelligent woman. She made it to the Midlands, but was not able to take hold of her life fully, and we lost touch with her. I don't know what she is doing now, but I know that my life was enriched by knowing her.

Many of the street-based sex workers coming into One25 have no reason to trust anybody, having suffered abuse and violence throughout their lives. It is therefore an enormous privilege to come alongside such women and earn their trust. This often takes years but it can also happen quite suddenly, at times of trauma, such as death of a partner, child, or parent.

It can also happen during pregnancy, when issues such as housing and drug dependency have to be faced. This can be particularly difficult for women who, for many reasons, no longer have contact with their families. It may be possible at these times to offer real support and encouragement, which quite possibly will be the only positive input in their lives.

I was privileged to be asked by one of our regular service users to be her birthing partner. This experience was, for me, more than a privilege. It was a very moving experience and stirred up a great concern within me for pregnant female sex workers, who often had no support from family and no safe home.

I received a telephone call from Tina and picked her up at 6.30 a.m. on a Sunday morning, taking her to St Michael's

Hospital. Tina was in the early stages of labour, but because there had been complications during the pregnancy she was being closely monitored. The midwife said we could go away and have some breakfast, but needed to return to the hospital in a couple of hours. Tina was unable to eat anything but we both enjoyed coffee in a local café before returning to the hospital.

Tina was admitted later that morning and, after several hours in labour, gave birth to a beautiful daughter. What a privilege it was for me to hold that child and pray over her as I thanked God for her safe delivery.

Life had its ups and major downs for Tina and her daughter over the next six years, as her use of crack cocaine affected her physical and mental health. There were times when I was frustrated by her lack of progress, and others when I was encouraged by positive change. I always kept praying for her. Fourteen years ago, Tina decided that enough was enough concerning her drug use, and she decided to stop. Without outside help from anyone, Tina stopped all use of crack cocaine. She went through emotional and physical pain – but she did it, and she is still drug-free now. I remain amazed at her strength and courage.

Since my retirement I have continued to support Tina and her family, and over the years this has changed to become a friendship of mutual support and love. Cliff has also become a trusted friend of Tina and her children, as well as being a wonderful role model of what a real man can be. I could never have foreseen this outcome all those years ago, when Tina was in the throes of drug dependency and homelessness, but I truly thank God that her life was turned around.

Tina still has to deal with the consequences of her long-term past drug use – her mind and body are still ravaged. Crack cocaine damages the pleasure receptors of your brain, so you never again experience pleasure or beauty like you once did. Things are not easy for Tina, but she has come through a huge amount in life, and she continues to press on.

Over the next few years, God would increasingly put on my heart the impact of criminal activity and drug dependency on families and children. One distressing conversation with a 9-year-old boy left me particularly shocked and broken-hearted.

I had received a telephone call one morning from Debbie, a mother of three boys, who was married to a drug user. The previous day Debbie's husband had been sent to prison, and she asked me to visit her at home. I arrived at the family home and was met at the front door by the eldest boy, who was 9 years of age. He invited me in and told me that I could deal with him from now on, as he was now head of the family.

I looked at his gorgeous, serious eyes and was shocked to the core. What a statement to hear from a young child, and what a responsibility for a 9-year-old to take upon himself.

Things did not go well in that family for the children, which is unsurprising. Debbie continued selling sex – it was the only way she knew to support her family. She engaged really positively with both One25 and Social Services while her husband was in prison, but we could see that life was nonetheless taking its toll on her mental and physical health.

You can't ever predict when change might happen, and sometimes you can barely believe it ever will. Debbie's husband returned home following his release from prison and continued his chaotic lifestyle, driven by drug use, making the lives of his wife and children immensely difficult and painful. It took several years of this, but eventually, Debbie decided that enough was enough. She took hold of her life and stopped sex working. She had never used Class A drugs herself, and she gave her husband an ultimatum – either he stopped his drug abuse, or he left their home. He decided upon the latter and left the family.

Debbie started volunteering with a local community group – she was honest with them about her background, and I provided a character reference. Through this group, she accessed educational courses, leading to employment. Debbie discovered the strong woman within her and threw off the victim of circumstances that she had become. When I last saw her, she positively glowed.

Quite soon after establishing the drop-in, we took the decision to have outings. We wanted to show the women a different side of life, outside the fairly narrow confines of St Paul's. I had always been so nourished by the outdoors. I wanted to be able to widen their horizons too, to feed a sense of hope, to show them more of what was out there in the wonderful world. Also, I just wanted to take these women and their children out, and treat them to a really good time.

Initially, these outings happened during the summer months. We would hire a coach and take the women and their children to Weston-super-Mare for the day. We usually met around 9.30 a.m. at the Grosvenor Centre for bacon butties before setting off with families, staff members and volunteers to Weston and the Tropicana.

The Tropicana – now sadly closed – was a large open-air swimming pool with a slide and a diving board, situated on the beach. It provided enormous fun for everyone. The women would often have tea or coffee and a pastry while their children tore around the slides and splashed in the pool. Then we would all move off to the beach for a picnic lunch, which we had prepared beforehand. Lunch was followed by fun on the beach, including rounders and various ball games, and also just relaxing and building sandcastles, for which the Weston sand is perfect.

The highlight of the day came around 5 p.m., when Chris and I would run off into the town to collect our previously ordered fish and chips. It was such a treat for all of us and an amazing opportunity to relax with the families and get to know them away from the streets of Bristol. There was always an enormous sense of joy and freedom.

Not to say that things didn't occasionally go wrong.

One of the trips to Weston-super-Mare had a rather tainted ending. The weather was perfect, swimming in the Tropicana was wonderful and we had enjoyed a picnic lunch on the beach. Chris and others organized a game of rounders with everyone, which was enormous fun, and then we collected people together to go to SeaQuarium. It was then, on a head count, that we realized we had 'lost' two adult women, and two children belonging to one of them.

Chris and I searched Weston beach and town, without success. We always gave all the women on the trip strict instructions about where to be, and what time, and the rest of the families were disgusted by the lack of respect shown by these two women.

At teatime, Chris and I headed off into the town as usual to collect fish and chips for everyone, and our coach came to collect us from the seafront at 6 p.m., but the shine had come off our outing. There was still no sign of our missing people. Our coach driver agreed to drive the length of the promenade and back through town as we searched the pavements, to no avail. Sadly, we concluded that we had to head home without

them. It left us with a sense of sadness and disappointment –
we felt let down, and were more than a little worried about
what had happened.

Later that evening, I was out on the van, and to my astonishment, one of the women whom we had lost in Weston
was working on the street, and came up for a drink and sandwich. When she saw me there was no sign of regret or apology.
Rather, she was cross that we had left them behind. 'Call yourself a Christian?' she accused. 'You abandoned me!'

I wasn't having that – I knew we had done all we possibly
could to find them so, desperate to remain calm, I said, 'No.
You left us.'

After a tense dialogue, she finally admitted that she and the
other woman had been arrested in Weston – for soliciting –
and detained for a while. I was terribly sad, particularly for
the two children involved. They were taken into care not long
after that incident.

The very best planning cannot take into account the English weather and the following was from a flyer advertising an
outing to Longleat safari park:

Are you coming to Longleat Wednesday 15th April 1998?
Safari Park
Adventure Playground
Train Rides
House
Lake & Gardens and much, much more!

Well, there certainly was much, much more. As our coach
approached the safari park, snow began to fall and this quickly
turned into a blizzard – in mid-April! This meant that an

outside picnic was out of the question, so we had to munch our sandwiches sitting in the coach. Even more memorable, perhaps, was the drive through the safari park past the lions, each with more than an inch of snow on their backs, poor creatures. They looked utterly miserable. Our children were unimpressed that the lions were not more active, and that the monkeys were shivering.

After a couple of years, we added a further outing to our schedule. This took place on the date of the One25 Christmas Party, usually the Saturday before Christmas Day, and together the outing and the party formed a whole day of Christmas celebrations.

We booked seats in the Bristol Old Vic for the matinee performance of the Christmas pantomime. It felt a bit risky at first, as many of the children were not used to being confined for any length of time, but they absolutely loved it. On one occasion, the actors invited our children onto the stage during the interval and handed them sweets.

At the end of the panto, we would head back to the Grosvenor Centre where a team of workers had prepared a special tea, with entertainment and face painting, and of course, Father Christmas with a gift for each child. This was followed by games – the favourite being a kind of musical chairs, but diving under a parachute. It was pretty exhausting, but such a joyous experience for all of us.

These outings often brought back to me how little our women had seen of the world, and how narrow their experience was – none more than our visit to the Royal Opera House, to see a ballet. Surely this must rank as our most adventurous outing! One morning in the post, I received from an anonymous donor a number of tickets for the Royal Opera

House, either for an opera or a ballet. These were tickets each costing £8 for the Orchestra Stalls, right at the bottom of the huge venue, close to the stage and at eye level.

We decided upon the ballet as being the best option, and so on 29 February 2000, we set off in a twenty-one-seater bus kindly loaned to us by Chris's church, St Philip & St James' Church in Bath. Chris and I shared the driving and with us were Helen and Pat, together with eight of the women. We left the Grosvenor Centre around 1 p.m. and stopped in a nice hotel in Windsor for a meal, which we had previously booked.

The hotel in Windsor was very welcoming, with a large log fire. This delighted the women, on a chilly February day, and before I knew it, they had rushed towards the fireplace, kicked off their shoes and lifted up their skirts, with their backs and bottoms to the fire, to feel its heat.

It made me quite emotional to see this – it was so natural, so girlish and free – it showed a sort of innocence which these women had been denied in life. That's what's so precious about just being women together. There's no power struggle; we were just women, equals and joyful.

We all consumed a delicious meal together before setting off for Covent Garden and the performance at 7.30 p.m. We had excellent seats and everything went well until the curtain went up, and the dancers appeared on the stage. The women had never seen a male ballet dancer, and were surprised to say the least, when they arrived in their very tight ballet tights. You can imagine, with our seats close to the stage, looking slightly up at the performers, the women had never seen anything like it!

They also weren't aware of the culture of respectful quiet which generally pervades the Royal Opera House, Covent

Garden. I've no idea whether the male dancers were at all put off by the squawks of surprise and barely muffled guffaws of laughter, but there was no hiding our group, as they fell about laughing in the centre of the theatre, in full view of the whole of the rest of the audience.

I was a little embarrassed, to say the least, but things did settle down, and they loved the ballet and the music.

The interval was another first experience for them, as we had pre-ordered tea, coffee and pastries. These were placed on a large table with our name, One25, clearly printed on an embossed card. This would be something many theatregoers wouldn't bat an eyelid at, but the women loved it. They felt known and valued, that this had all been prearranged and provided especially for them.

On the way home we stopped off in a motorway service station and produced a good picnic supper, which was also much appreciated. We arrived back at the Grosvenor Centre around 1 a.m., which was twelve hours after we had left. What an uplifting experience that was for us all, and so rewarding. However, this was the sad part – to say goodbye to our eight companions of the day, those brilliantly funny and natural women, and to see them going out onto the streets to work.

Years later, when outings were being discussed and arranged with some of the women, one lady in particular would *always* tell the story of our trip to the Royal Opera House in Covent Garden to see the ballet, and recount with glee the men with their very tight tights! The story was generally received with total disbelief by others listening, but this lady could assure them that she had seen it all, with her very own eyes.

13

Tiny White Coffin

In May 1998, the management team took the decision that One25 should have an external audit in order to ensure that our service was appropriate and delivered well. We approached Teela Sanders, who was a student in the Department of Applied Social Studies, University of Oxford, reading for an MSc with a Diploma in Social Work. Teela had experience of working with women who sold sex, and needed to carry out research for her diploma. This matched up well with our aim of having One25's service evaluated objectively.

The fieldwork was conducted throughout August 1998, with thirty-two interviews carried out with working women. They were each paid a small amount to answer ten questions. Of the thirty-two interviews, twenty-seven were carried out on the van outreach, and five in the Grosvenor Centre drop-in.

Teela's audit was illuminating in a number of ways. It showed how organizations such as One25 need to listen to the people they hope to reach. For us, it also emphasized what an effective service the van provided, and just how valued it was by the women. One of the questions Teela asked was, 'What impact would it have if the van was to stop tomorrow?' The following are the women's responses, in their own words:

- *'It would be less safe for the girls and we wouldn't know what was happening in different streets.'* [Often, on the van, the women swapped information about where was a safe place to work that night, or which areas to avoid.]
- *'****** hell – it would be terrible . . . it's a good thing . . . we would have no condoms, and life on the street would be worse. Some of the girls only eat when the van is around.'*
- *'There would be more violence and AIDS – Durex are really important.'*
- *'The van is great – I would miss the conversation and atmosphere, everyone is so down to earth. When we see the van, you know there will be some friendly faces, gives us security where you're out there.'*
- *'It would be such a downer' . . . 'Work would be depressing' . . . 'Devastating' . . . 'I would starve.'*

By 1998, client-based work was expanding very rapidly. Women were requesting advocacy and support during court attendances, and this extended to prison and hospital visiting. The management team took the very welcome decision to appoint Helen Hill to our team of paid workers. Helen, with her legal experience, was hugely helpful in working with families, especially where there were issues raised by Social Services concerning children's safety. In addition, Helen undertook fundraising, which was a massive help to me and to the development of One25. Helen brought her own gentle but firm personality to the project and was a great asset. Helen, Chris and I provided the stability and core team for the developing project.

Early on in our van outreach, women would get on the van and tell us of violent attacks, some of which had just happened. It was decided that we should have a form of reporting these acts of violence to the police. We designed an A4 form, with the outline of a figure on it, which could be filled in with distinguishing features of the attacker. These 'ugly mugs', as they became known, became valuable to the police in identifying perpetrators.

There was always learning to be done, however. In some cases, the women were unable to fill in the forms themselves, so our team members helped them write or draw their evidence. We discovered that these particular descriptions did not stand up in court, due to the impression that the volunteers might have put their own gloss on the facts. It was therefore essential that the exact words used by the victims of violence were always used, and that we did not use our own language to describe the offence or to make any suggestions at all to the victim regarding either the offence or the perpetrator's appearance.

Sadly, because violence is such a widespread feature of life for women in sex work, supporting them in both crown and magistrates' courts was, and remains, an important part of One25's role. In particular, women were very reluctant to report rape. After all, who would believe a sex worker that they had been raped? Many times in Crown Court, I heard the defence lawyer claim that the sex had been consensual even though there were often injuries and evidence that this had not been the case. The whole experience for victims of rape and violent assault was traumatic, and all too often the perpetrator would walk free.

In one such case where this happened, as the victim and I walked back to her home afterwards, her only words to me were, 'Never ask me to do that again. I feel as though I have been raped all over again.'

That woman had suffered appalling injuries and had been supported by ourselves and Avon and Somerset Police in her claim of rape. However, once the jury heard the opening remarks from the defending barrister, justice was hard to achieve, and the defendant ended up walking free. The barrister had started with the words, 'This woman is a common prostitute, and a drug addict.'

Because of One25's experience of working with female sex workers, we were invited by the Magistrates Association in Bristol to give some training in the issues involved. Helen, Chris and I went along and spoke to a large group of magistrates. I was able to explain the complex issues faced by the women, and how these affected their ability to take part in court proceedings. One25 continues to be a regular provider of training both to Bristol magistrates and to the police. Thankfully, much is changing in terms of rape cases, but there is still a long way to go.

Prison visiting was an important part of our work with women, who could find themselves jailed for drug offences, violence or other offences. Visiting supported both the prisoner and her family. It gave the opportunity to engage with the woman herself at a deep level, as she took stock of her life from behind bars, or even considered a life without drugs. It also sometimes gave opportunities to link with families, which was extremely helpful upon release from prison.

Release from prison is a defining moment for someone's life, when the balance can tip either way. This is the point at which it can be possible for men and women to make positive changes to their lives, but it is also a time of great vulnerability. High on the list of needs for prisoners upon discharge is safe housing. Without somewhere safe to go, they easily become homeless again, and part of the street scene of drug and alcohol abuse.

It was always part of our support package to be at the prison gates for a woman prisoner being discharged. This was usually around 8 a.m., and we also hoped to take them to a safe address and to link with any other support agencies for ongoing care. Sometimes this was possible. Sometimes we watched helplessly as their old life sucked them back in again.

Betty's life had spiralled out of control, and she was sent to Eastwood Park prison when she was already pregnant. She contacted us to let us know that she had been safely delivered of twin girls while in jail. Then, not long afterwards, I received another telephone call from her in prison. This call was to ask for support at the funeral of one of the babies, who had died a cot death. I remember her voice showed no emotion, she simply asked me to meet her at the chapel for the service, followed by the burial.

I shall never forget that morning. Betty arrived with her right arm handcuffed to a prison warder. I sat alongside her to the left, and we three were the only mourners present in the crematorium. The service was short but meaningful, and we then made our way to the graveside. I still have a vivid memory of the tiny white coffin being lowered into the ground. Betty again showed little emotion. I cannot imagine the grief and emotion she suffered once she was back in her prison cell, alone with the surviving twin.

Sadly, this took place around eleven years ago and I understand that Betty is still living a chaotic life, her surviving daughter having been adopted.

Even as One25 was going from strength to strength, my heart was beginning to ache for pregnant women, and those with small babies, who were navigating life through the chaos of sex work, drug dependency and homelessness. They needed more than a drop-in or a van. They needed stability, somewhere to live safely, the ability to make positive choices for their families, away from the madness of their street-based lives. How can anyone rebuild their lives if they have no safe accommodation – somewhere to get their head together?

Added to the lack of housing is the need for drug and alcohol treatment and rehabilitation, together with help in working through the effects of long-term abuse and violent relationships. Time and again, we met women who were pregnant but had insufficient support and/or housing for themselves and their new baby. This would often end up with the baby being taken away from the mother into care very soon after being born. The needs of the child are paramount, but this is still tragic to witness, especially if you feel the mother could take good care of her baby, if given the support and wherewithal to do so.

In July 2000, two local doctors conducted a health needs assessment of seventy-one female sex workers in Bristol during a one-month period in July 2000. This research would be published in the *Journal of Public Health* in 2004.[3] Among other things, the researchers found that:

- 62% of the women interviewed had experienced physical, sexual or emotional abuse as a child;
- 38% had been in care;

- 32% left full time education aged 14 or younger, with women who had been in care leaving significantly younger;
- 66% were homeless or under threat of homelessness. They stayed in B&Bs, on floors of friends or clients, hostels, crack houses, or slept rough;
- 51% had started working in prostitution to fund a drug habit;
- 20% had been forced into prostitution by a partner;
- 96% had current drug or alcohol dependency problems, with 60% of those injecting;
- 83% used heroin, and of these, 81% also used crack cocaine;
- 22% of injecting drug users had shared needles in the previous 4 weeks, and 59% had shared other injecting equipment, despite 96% considering this a risk;
- 73% experienced violence. Assault, including rape and use of weapons such as guns, machetes and chainsaws, had been experienced.

It is clear from these shocking statistics that the needs of female sex workers were both complex and urgent and this really focused my mind concerning the need for safe housing. My experience, and that of other workers in the field, was that the majority of the women we met and engaged with, on the van or in the drop-in, were without hope. This was something that saddened us very much as we could see the potential they couldn't see. We longed to help these women to live fulfilled lives.

Many, though by no means all, of the men and women I have met who are abusing alcohol or drugs have a family history of abuse, so the statistics in the journal made tragic sense to me. This childhood abuse can take the form of neglect, physical and/or sexual abuse, and mental abuse and is often linked to parental alcohol or drug misuse. Not only are children in the family harmed, but they also go through their early life without any good role models of what a loving, protecting parent would be like.

The police and social workers, as well as school teachers, are well aware of families where more than one generation is severely affected by the results of drug and alcohol abuse. However, working with these families is easier said than done. I witnessed social workers trying hard with a particular family who were known to One25. There were four children in this family, all suffering neglect and physical abuse due to the mother's dependence on crack cocaine. The two fathers of the children were mostly absent, except for occasional periods when one of them returned home temporarily, and was violent towards the mother. This was often witnessed by the children.

This particular mother resisted letting social workers into the family home, although the children remained in her care. One of the daughters, the second eldest child, was seen working on the streets of Bristol but refused to engage with staff, and the youngest son became the victim of a serious stabbing, leaving him with injuries for life.

The eldest son, however, had a very contrasting experience. He had spent the majority of his life living with his grandmother, who provided a loving and caring home. I last saw him in his early adulthood, coming down the escalator in a department store! He spotted me and waved. Then, on reaching the shop floor, he ran across and gave me a warm hug. He looked happy and well, and told me he was in a stable relationship. It was wonderful to see him, but so challenging to observe the difference between him and his siblings, who had not had the stable care he had enjoyed.

I can well understand why people who have suffered abuse as children turn to mind-altering drugs such as heroin or alcohol. They are, in fact, self-medicating to cope with the pain. However, these painkillers are also deadly, and this ends up perpetuating the cycle of abuse, violence and hurt.

Many drug support workers will have had conversations with young people who have had the responsibility not only of obtaining drugs for their parents, but of actually injecting them with heroin or cocaine. The obvious next step for those young people is to use the drug of choice themselves.

We were failing these children and families through a lack of understanding, and through the lack of the resources to really get alongside them and provide support and help in a structured, ongoing way.

No one agency could provide each stage of recovery but I was starting to see very clearly that there was a need for a sort of 'pathway' to recovery – where each step, each piece of support provided, worked together to create the possibility for positive change, rather than a vicious circle of failure.

What if we could get alongside women, and walk this whole pathway with them?

In the year 2000, One25 was one of ten national winners of an IMPACT Award – an award scheme for community and voluntary organizations, funded by GlaxoSmithKline and The King's Fund. The awards are still running today.

The IMPACT Awards are designed to 'recognise and promote the work of voluntary organisations with a proven track record in the challenging and demanding area of community healthcare'.[4] The excellent administration skills of Helen Hill, and Dorothy Milne's medical expertise, were both crucial in securing us this award. The criteria used to assess applications included innovation, management, partnership, community focus and the way in which the organization targeted a particular need.

The award brought in £25,000 for One25, as well as unmeasurable respect and esteem for the project, which was a brilliantly professional and effective outfit by this time. The judges commended One25 on targeting a high-risk group, and providing them with a 'superb service'. They recognized our increasing involvement with other local and national agencies and that we were even getting involved in policy formation.

The judges expressed a hope that the IMPACT Award would provide an independent mark of approval and encouragement for our project. It certainly did. It also meant a huge amount to our staff, our volunteers and to the women as well. They were immensely proud that One25 had won the award, and you could see that it made them feel valued.

I was over the moon when we won the award. But something else was happening too.

Inside, I was churning with ideas about mothers, children, families, and a care pathway. Meanwhile, One25 was being recognized as a professional organization, becoming more well known, established and respected. With that came skilled people, funding, recognition, resources and a steady stream of wonderful volunteers.

Was it possible that One25 had now become an organization separate from my own involvement? Was it conceivable that I myself might not always be needed?

14

Retreats and Advances

Back in Chicago, at Genesis House, I had met a lovely Catholic nun, Sister Olga MacDougal. She worked for a couple of years in the 'Windy City' before returning to her convent in Nova Scotia. We had kept in touch following my return home, and at some point, Olga had given me an invitation to take a retreat at her convent. In September 2001, I took up her invitation, and travelled for a two-week silent retreat in the convent in Antigonish.

It was both wonderful and painful. Wonderful because the convent is situated in the open countryside with eagles and bears and a river with snapper turtles. Painful because, as the days passed, I knew I was being led to lay down One25 and retire.

'But what then?' I heard myself asking, almost frantically. I had a real sense of needing to let go of One25, but like any mother hen, I found it hard to do so.

I spent my days out in the countryside with sandwiches, an apple and my Bible, enthralled by the bald eagles which went swooping over my head to their eyrie nearby. I experienced peace during that retreat as I communed with nature, and just breathed in the beauty of God's creation.

I was blissfully unaware of the danger of bears, though apparently the nuns were quite anxious about my safety. I did have one lucky escape when I attempted to rescue a little turtle I came across on a path alongside a flooded river. Snapping turtles were not something I had encountered previously, and I thought it was a cute, harmless little thing until I tried to pick it up and it attempted to snap off my finger. I dropped it in the river in the nick of time.

I returned home and confirmed to the management team my decision to retire. I was 60 and had led One25 for five years. They accepted my decision to retire, although they did ask if I would take on a voluntary role instead, and also offered me a position as a trustee of the charity. However, I felt it was right to completely let go at that point. I turned down these offers and retired early in 2002.

New skills were needed to take the organization forward – professional skills which I did not have. I recognized the need for social work experience, to continue giving credibility, especially in our partnerships with statutory organizations. I had been the right person to start One25, but I wasn't the right person to continue it. The truth was, I was an amateur, a visionary, a jack-of-all-trades, just someone who had said, 'Here I am, God, use me.' God had indeed used me, immensely, and now was the time to move on.

At home, I quickly ran out of those jobs I had long wanted to do but not had the time for. The days seemed endless and empty. I plummeted into depression and a loss of identity. I'd been so closely identified with One25 that it sometimes felt like my name was actually Val-Jeal-from-One-Two-Five. Who was I now? And what could I do with the remainder of my life? Who would want me, and to do what? I needed to find Val again.

The first nine months of 2002 were spent in a deep depression with panic attacks. This was different from the breakdown I'd had after the Candle Project, when I'd gone to Genesis House. That was a total loss of power, energy, vision and physical will. I had been completely exhausted, worn out, used up in body and spirit. I felt empty.

This time, I was physically healthy, had the vision, the desire, even the energy, in a way, but I had lost my hope. I felt pointless.

Last time, there was failure – my kicking of Jan, and the closing of our initial women's drop-in. This time there was success – the work was flourishing, growing, winning awards. In fact, it was doing so well, that it didn't need me any more . . .

I had experienced depression years earlier during and after the break-up of my first marriage. This time – ironically – it was exacerbated by the fact that I had become a Christian and felt I should not be experiencing depression. Rather, I should be trusting in God. The truth was, I could not feel any trust in God, or in myself, or in anyone else. There just seemed to be endless darkness. I found it impossible to motivate myself. It was too easy to just pull the sheets up over my head and spend hours in bed – unable to sleep but also unable to get up.

I did not want to take antidepressants. On a visit to the GP, he had raised his eyebrows while reading my record on the screen, and sighed, 'I see you have a long history of depression.' I didn't have a long history of depression – I had been depressed once before, a long time ago – coming out of a harmful marriage. I felt labelled and looked down upon, and didn't go back.

Prayer was impossible, and I seemed unable to hear God. I was also unable to seek help. The depression reached a climax one August lunchtime. I had a frightening panic attack and felt truly afraid. Never before had I bothered Cliff during his working day, but on this occasion, I rang him in the Bristol University Pathology Department, and asked if he could come home, quickly. Cliff returned home to me and helped to calm me down. Without the love and support of Cliff, I really do not know how I would have ever got through those dark days and months of depression. He was wonderfully supportive and encouraging. We were sharing a cup of tea together when the telephone rang and Cliff answered it.

The caller was an unknown lady ringing from South Wales. She was called Sally, and owned a property in Bristol. Sally was looking for someone to act as caretaker of her property, and to open it up several days each week to run a cooked lunch service for homeless people. Someone had given her my name as a possibility.

Someone wanted me.

I had not expected to be wanted again.

Sally invited me to have lunch with her in the property, and to discuss what she had in mind. We agreed to meet the following week. When we did, Sally took me on a tour of the building, which was a large disused church and church hall. The duties of caretaker would include caring for the fabric of the buildings, she told me, which I immediately recognized was beyond me. I said I would pray about her proposal but from the start I did not feel it was something I either wanted to take on, or was capable of doing.

I did manage to pray about Sally's offer over the next few days, but even though I was desperate to do something, I had no clear indication from God that this was it. I rang Sally and thanked her, but said it was not a job I wanted to take. However, I did explain that just by contacting me, she had given me hope for the future at a time when I had no hope. My confidence was tentatively boosted.

During the late summer, I reconnected with One25 as a volunteer team leader/driver on the outreach van. This was meaningful and helped me feel useful. It also kept me in contact with the women I still cared about.

I started to develop a training role as I went out on the van – I talked through with new volunteers what to look out for on the streets, how to assess different situations, and spot potential danger. I taught them how to speak appropriately and accessibly to the women they would meet, and when to leave space in case a women wanted to talk in her own time. This reminded me of just how much I had learned over the years, and it was a great privilege to pass the learning on.

As I reflect on the two occasions when I have suffered from depression, I realize that there was something very particular each time that kept me holding on. In the depression surrounding the break-up of my first marriage and the two years following that, I clearly remember that my reason for living was my son, David. My love for him was strong and gave me a purpose in life. David needed me, and I needed David.

During the shorter, but intense depression following retirement from One25, I found joy in David's daughter, my beautiful 2-year-old granddaughter, Hannah. Hannah was a gift during a dark time. She was, and is, very special to Cliff and to me and has always given us much joy.

How much more do women on the streets yearn for that relationship of love with their own child, in the chaos and difficulty of their lives?

I received a telephone call early in 2002 from Sister Annaliese to tell me of a meeting that I should attend with her. A Catholic priest by the name of Father Richard McKay was the priest at St Nicholas of Tolentino, Easton, in inner-city Bristol. He was holding a public meeting to discuss the plight of male ex-offenders upon leaving prison. Many of these men called at his inner-city presbytery asking for a sandwich and a cup of tea and spoke of their need for shelter and some hope for the future.

Annaliese and I attended the meeting, which was fascinating and packed with people. Father Richard put the case strongly for accommodation to be provided for these men immediately when they left prison, and before they hit the streets of Bristol and went back into old behaviours and drug/alcohol abuse. Everything he said was spot on, but he only spoke about the needs of male ex-offenders. Something in me stirred and I began, from the back of the hall, to heckle, saying, 'How about the women?'

After several attempts at getting Father Richard's attention, he addressed me, saying, 'The lady at the back, I will speak to you after the meeting ends!' True to his word, he did so, and this was the beginning of a productive relationship with this man of God, who really cared about people on the margins.

Father Richard and I would eventually work together to provide supported accommodation, with a care pathway for both men and women. At that stage, though, neither of us had much idea how or when we could make this happen!

Still in the midst of my difficult period of depression, Father Richard introduced me to Alabaré Christian Care Centres, who were based in Salisbury, Wiltshire. This organization already ran several hostels for homeless men and women in the West of England. We hoped that it might be possible in the future to work with Alabaré in Bristol.

After my rather rude heckling of his meeting, Father Richard also most generously agreed that if we were able to work together to secure supported housing, then the first home would be for female sex workers who were committed to change. We even decided on the name of this house – it would be called The Well. It would be a place where people could drink deep of life-giving water.

A couple of months later, on a Tuesday morning in October 2002, I received a telephone call from the vice liaison officer of Avon and Somerset Police. This officer knew of my desire to see supported housing set up for women sex workers who were considering change. She told me that there was 'money sloshing around' from recovered assets – funds recovered from convicted big-time drug dealers. The officer gave me a telephone number to call, which was the South West office of the Home Office.

I rang the number and spoke to the person there. He told me that there was, indeed, money available as a grant, but that I was much too late to apply for it. The closing date was twelve noon on the Friday of that very week. Three days away. I found myself saying that was not a problem and could he give me more details, please? I was told to collect the necessary forms needed for the grant application that afternoon, which I did.

I then rang a lady who also volunteered with One25 and had experience of fundraising. She agreed to meet me later that afternoon and immediately we started work on preparing an application for the whole £100,000 available from the fund. We worked Tuesday evening, then all day Wednesday and Thursday, and I took the completed grant application forms to the Bristol office of the Home Office at 11.50 a.m. on Friday of that week, the closing date. It was accepted, but I was told it might take a while to make a decision.

I was at home one evening, in the first week of November 2002, getting ready to go out to the van outreach. It was a cold night, and I was about to put on my puffer coat and boots. My rucksack was packed with sandwiches and goodies. The telephone rang and I answered, thinking that perhaps one of the other volunteers was unable to make it. I was surprised that the caller was Sister Paul, a Catholic nun who I had met when she was the chaplain in HMP Eastwood Park.

Sister Paul told me that she knew of my desire for provision of a safe house for female sex workers wanting change, and that she had arranged for me to meet a man 'with access to funding'. The meeting, she told me, had been arranged for 8 p.m. that evening. That was the time when I should be meeting my team of volunteers to go on outreach in the van. I tried to explain this to Sister Paul, but she insisted that the meeting had been arranged and I should go. I contacted the two volunteers to let them know that I would be late in arriving for outreach and set off to meet this Catholic businessman.

The businessman, Mr Murray, received me with grace but was also slightly ruffled at being told to meet me as he, too, had had other plans at 8 p.m. that evening! He asked me to state my request clearly and swiftly, which I did. I told him of the grant application to the Home Office and of a property I had seen which was coming up for auction and needed repairs and renovation to make it suitable. Mr Murray asked how we would repay a loan if he decided to give us one, and I said that I was hopeful that churches in the city would respond if I was able to go and speak to them about the project. I also mentioned that I was in touch with Father Richard, and this seemed to carry weight. I left him to think about it, and headed off for my delayed van outreach.

A couple of days later, I received a telephone call from Mr Murray agreeing to attend the auction of the house I had identified, and to give us a loan payable over three years. He stipulated that in the auction he would not go above £100,000, this being the maximum grant from the Home Office that we had applied for. The property had been valued at between £120,000 – £140,000. However, once again we were to experience generosity beyond and above. Mr Murray agreed that if he was successful in purchasing the property, he would rent it to us on a peppercorn rent of £1 per year for three years! 'Here we go again,' I thought. It had all the hallmarks of God's planning – all the excitement of what might be, but also all the scariness of another new voyage into the unknown.

The grant application decision was due in the second week of November, and the auction was in the same week. Somehow, I had also managed to book to go on an eight-day silent retreat, beginning that very same week! So off I went to the Community of the Sisters of the Church in Ham, Surrey, leaving Cliff probably quite happy not to have me around the house in a state of extreme, agitated anticipation!

I can remember my spiritual director in Ham, Sister Aileen, encouraging me to spend plenty of time in my room, being quiet and still. Impossible! I managed to stay quiet, but there was too much to think about and too much nervous energy for me to remain in my room. Instead, I pounded the paths of nearby Richmond Park, my mind a swirl of prayers and plans. I tried not to frighten the deer.

15

The Well

Finally, the last morning of the retreat arrived and Cliff drove to Ham to bring me home. As soon as I got in the car, I inundated him with questions about my email. Was there a message from the Home Office? Was there a message from Mr Murray about the auction? My head was buzzing but Cliff, his usual calm self, told me to wait until I arrived home!

The minute I arrived, I dashed upstairs to our computer and my email messages. Yes! The Home Office grant application had been successful and we were awarded the full £100,000. Then I read the conditions, and gasped. It was the third week of November 2002. The condition of the grant was that all the money – all £100,000 – had to be spent, and the project had to be up and running, by 1 March 2003.

The next email in my inbox was from Mr Murray. He had successfully bid for the property in Easton and was willing to go ahead with our project – a safe home for female sex workers committed to change, where they would be able to access the care and support they needed. The Well.

I sat there in our upstairs room at home, looking at the computer screen and brimming with joy. At last, I could start planning the reality of an idea that had been forming in my mind for years. This would be a smaller-scale project than One25, but with a much more intensive structure. My hope was that for women at the right stage, with the right mindset, we could help break the chains of abuse.

Not only would they have a home – a safe, secure and supportive environment – but they would also have access, through the home, to counselling, practical help and emotional support. They would be given a real chance to address the issues that had resulted in substance abuse and their sex work, and they could begin to turn their lives around.

We received the keys to the property on 20 December 2002. There was so much to do in such a short space of time. Father Richard arranged a meeting with Alabaré Christian Care Centres, together with a number of people we felt would be helpful and supportive in moving things forward. Alabaré Christian Care Centres were brilliant. They agreed to take on the management of The Well and advised on policies and procedures. I agreed to get tenders for the building work, which was essential before any residents could move in. We also needed to recruit staff and have time to train them – all in just three months!

Alabaré Christian Care Centres took responsibility for the payroll and advertising for staff. Their experience of managing residential accommodation in Wiltshire was indispensable. It was agreed that a regional office of Alabaré would be set up in Bristol, and an Alabaré Bristol Group established.

This was particularly helpful because, in addition to The Well, Mr Murray had also agreed to help financially in setting up the original house that Father Richard had hoped for – a home for male ex-offenders. In the end, Lazarus House would be founded at almost exactly the same time as The Well. Our heads were spinning, and it was so good to have Alabaré's practical and management experience.

The property which was to be The Well was an early 1900s four-bed detached house in a quiet residential area of Easton. It had a small, high-walled garden to the rear, which meant it was contained and safe. At the bottom of the garden was a garage, which we would be able to convert into a fifth bedroom. The house had not been updated for a long time and needed much renovation and restoration, but in all other ways it was perfect.

We settled upon a local builder and building work began at the beginning of January 2003. Two en-suite bathrooms were fitted in residents' rooms, and the existing bathroom was completely renovated. The gas boiler and the electrics were all replaced. The kitchen ceiling had to be replaced too, all the kitchen units taken out and new ones put in, and a modern cooker installed. A small office was created out of the hall space, and a small 'containment' area just inside the front door, making entry safe. All downstairs windows had bullet-proof glass fitted. We weren't expecting to be shot at, but it was the strongest glass you could get. All windows were also fitted with safety catches, and CCTV was installed overlooking front and rear doors.

I met with local residents to inform them that a home for a small number of vulnerable women would be opening, and reassured them that this should not cause any problem locally.

A newly appointed manager, Helen, started work on 6 January 2003. Bristol City Council agreed to meet the full cost of each resident's Housing Benefit, to a total of £850 per resident, per week, for a three-year period – with certain targets to be reached as a condition of funding. This would be a substantial help towards the staffing cost of the manager, the overnight sleep-in cover and a daytime resettlement worker.

The last day of February 2003 arrived, and the builders were still working flat out to finish their work. The Home Office grant depended on the project being open and working on 1 March 2003. It was going to be a close thing. Everything was in place to meet a pregnant woman from HMP Eastwood Park the following morning at 8 a.m., and bring her to The Well on her release. But first – we had to get a room ready for her.

Only one bedroom was finished and ready for occupation at that point. I telephoned members of my church home-group to ask for help in assembling furniture purchased from IKEA, and in cleaning the room. Wonderfully, they all agreed to come, and together we worked literally through the night. We washed the windows, cleaned the floor, fitted a curtain rail, hung the curtains and put together the furniture – bed, wardrobe and chest of drawers. Finally, we made the bed with sheets, duvet and pillows, and put the finishing touches to the room. It looked a treat. This was the green room, with matching curtains, duvet cover and towels. I insisted that there was nice soap in the bathroom, and also some pyjamas and a dressing gown for each woman who arrived. Everything was new and the best we could afford. The women were to be valued and this was where it started. If things went as hoped, this could be the beginning of a new life of choice and control for each resident.

Our little group of night-time workers, including Cliff and me, shared breakfast and prayed together. Then they headed off to work, or home, and I drove to Eastwood Park prison to collect Thelma, at 8 a.m. on 1 March 2003.

As we drove away from the prison, Thelma said she was excited to be going to The Well, but nervous about the future. She had detoxed from drug abuse while in prison, but had no family support or home to go to.

The Well was set up for single, homeless female sex workers, and we were unable to support babies or children. This was going to be an issue for Thelma, who was seven months pregnant at the time of her arrival, but we hoped to keep her safe until the birth of her baby, and provide help with rehousing at that point.

All residents in The Well were expected to remain clean of drugs and alcohol. This was a decision Father Richard and I made together, and we were both very certain that this was the right way to operate. Some facilities will tolerate some consumption of alcohol, or a level of drug use, or methadone – but we wanted men and women to be in their right minds. We felt only this would give them the best opportunity to take hold of their lives, and to hear God and respond to him. It also made the house safer for all the residents and staff.

This policy was made clear to the women before they were accepted into The Well, so we only took residents who were fully signed up to it. During their stay, they would be randomly tested for both drugs and alcohol, and risked being evicted if they had relapsed and lost motivation to change – although eviction wasn't automatic. This was an expensive policy, as drug tests cost quite a lot of money, but it was vital as part of The Well's structure for support and change, so it was very worthwhile.

Thelma and I arrived at The Well shortly after 9am and I accompanied her inside the house, parts of which were still pretty much like a building site. However, as she met Helen, the manager, and we showed her the bedroom, she exclaimed, 'Oh this is ******* beautiful!' and threw herself onto the newly made bed. It was a truly moving experience for Helen and me – to see how much it meant to Thelma to have a beautiful, welcoming home. It was exactly what we had wanted.

Thelma settled in quickly to her temporary home and initially remained clean. However, about a month into her stay, she was tested and showed to have used drugs. Thelma was challenged about this, but before we could talk it through fully, she decided that she would leave The Well. She went upstairs to her room and appeared shortly afterwards carrying a bin liner with her belongings in it. It was awfully sad to see her leave in this way. She had nowhere to go to, was heavily pregnant, and had used heroin.

Shortly after Thelma's departure, a member of staff and I went up to her room to clean it, and were disappointed to see that she had taken with her all the bedding and towels. I remember feeling sad that she had left in this way, but understood her motives for doing so. If you have nothing, and believe that no one cares about you, then why would you care about their stuff – why wouldn't you just see an opportunity to sell something for a few pounds, which might help get you your next fix?

About an hour after Thelma's departure the doorbell rang, and there she was again, still with the binbag of stuff. She said she had left something in her room and asked if she could get it. We said yes. Minutes later, Thelma came downstairs and left the house once again. We immediately checked her room and to our surprise, she had returned the bedding and towels. We were so pleased. Even though she had gone, Thelma had now left on good terms, leaving the way open for engaging with her in the future, as and when we could.

Indeed, I did engage with Thelma in the months to come. We heard that she had given birth to her baby, which was removed into care while she was still in hospital. Then her mental health deteriorated, to the extent that she was sectioned for her own safety. It was at this point that she contacted me and asked for a visit. During our conversation Thelma asked me to help her write her story, which we started but never finished. Over the coming months, and with the approval of her mental health doctor, I collected material from her and typed it up. Thelma's life had been a tale of abuse, neglect and violence from an early age, culminating in serious mental health issues.

Then on one visit, she suddenly announced that she no longer wanted to continue her writing, or see me any more. Sometime later I saw her again, when I was on the van outreach. She was clearly mentally unstable, and did not want to engage at all. I never saw her after that and have no idea what happened to her. I had respect for her, but also fear of her erratic and unstable behaviour when using mind-altering drugs. Thelma left a lasting impression on me and I would love to know what happened to her. There was an inner beauty in her that she seldom revealed – but it was there.

The Well was unique in the country in being specifically for street-based female sex workers and chaotic drug users who were motivated to change. Women were assessed in prison and were either met at the prison gates or the train station on their release. Without this facility they would most certainly have re-entered criminality, prostitution and drug abuse within hours.

Every woman who came to The Well had decided they wanted to change their life, and we designed our support to help them make this a reality. But I had learned back at the

Candle Project that you can never make someone change, you can only offer the chance, and make it as possible as you can for them. Many – indeed most – of the women who came to The Well were able to take the chance they were offered. What a privilege it was to see women able to make fundamental changes to their lives that would help them to realize their dreams and forge a future where they could reach their full potential.

Each of the five residents in The Well was expected to take part in an individually tailored programme of rehabilitation, to address the issues which had led to their drug/alcohol abuse and sex working. In addition, residents were expected to keep the house clean and tidy and to attend professional appointments such as health and housing. The atmosphere in the house was relaxed but orderly, as residents were encouraged to take responsibility for their lives and to gently plan for the future – a future without drugs or alcohol.

The women loved the fact that we'd put in bullet-proof glass – so they knew they were safe, secure. They loved the garden too, and would often sit out when the weather was good. The small pleasure of sitting in the garden to drink a cup of coffee was enormous to them.

It was encouraging to see women take hold of their lives, and move on to more independent living, with the ability to receive ongoing support from the staff team at The Well. Here is how one former resident described her experience:

The biggest thing for me was having somewhere safe to stay away from the streets and madness. I needed clear, strong boundaries to enable me to make the right choices. I stayed six months and gave birth to a premature baby. The staff were understanding and supportive during the five weeks after my son's birth until he left hospital and we moved together to our own home. Six months on we are doing well and being supported by The Well.

For many women, the small size and family feel of The Well were crucial in helping them feel secure enough to start making positive decisions about their lives. One woman contrasted this with the large hostels which were otherwise the only option available. These were generally not drug-free, so it was harder to stay clean. They were also normally for both men and women. This was very difficult for many women, for whom the coercive influence of men was a key factor in their lack of control.

In September 2003, one of the women we knew from the streets of Bristol was kidnapped. She was not working at the time but had gone out at night to the local garage to buy cigarettes. A car drew alongside her and asked for business. Carmen said that she was not working and started to walk away. The driver of the car persisted and eventually got out and forcibly pushed Carmen into the car, locking the doors. Carmen was taken to his home and kept there for six days. During that time she was repeatedly raped and suffered physical and mental abuse. The perpetrator burned her with cigarettes on a number of occasions. Finally, one evening he dumped Carmen in a multistorey car park in the centre of the city having tried to strangle her with his belt.

Amazingly, the police carried out a random check on the car park later that same evening and found Carmen unconscious and clothed in just a T-shirt. The police rushed her to Bristol Royal Infirmary, where she remained for several weeks.

During this time of recovery from her injuries, the police vice liaison officer rang me and asked if we had a room in

The Well available for Carmen when she left hospital. Thankfully, this was possible and upon discharge from hospital in mid-October 2003, I took Carmen straight to The Well where she began her recovery.

The Well was perfect for Carmen. She was part of a small community, with close-by help and support. She felt physically safe there, and free from negative influences. She loved having her own en suite bathroom, and also enjoyed sitting in our walled garden when it was sunny. Tiny step by tiny step, she moved forward in her physical and mental recovery. She started going on small shopping trips to the international food shops nearby, and the Bristol Sweet Mart. She also stayed drug-free from when she arrived from the hospital, right through her stay. At one point, we had a visit from the Lord Mayor and his wife, who presented the residents with certificates marking how long they had been clean. Carmen was particularly proud to receive her certificate, and became confident in telling other visitors how well she was doing. She also began building some of the skills she would need to move on to more independent housing.

Carmen was able to give the police the identity and address of the perpetrator of the crime and he eventually stood trial in the Crown Court, where he received a hefty prison sentence.

The vice liaison officer contacted Carmen and me to encourage Carmen to apply for criminal injuries compensation, in view of the seriousness of the trauma she had suffered. I subsequently helped Carmen with the application to the Criminal Injuries Compensation Authority (CICA), and enclosed with it a supporting letter, setting out how determined Carmen was to take hold of her life.

The application for compensation was refused because of her 'character as shown by criminal convictions or other evidence'.

Carmen did indeed have a number of previous convictions, which were listed by the CICA, the majority of which were for 'failing to surrender to custody at the appointed time' and theft – shoplifting. We noted that a number of these offences were committed while Carmen was still a minor, and when I challenged her, she admitted that she had stolen food as a child because she and her siblings were hungry. Carmen's early life was one of neglect and abuse, as her mother was a drug user.

I contacted our local Labour MP for Bristol West, Valerie Davey, who replied that she was 'concerned and saddened to read the correspondence' and wrote, 'If you feel that there is anything I can help with please do not hesitate to come back to me.' I also wrote to Caroline Flint MP, who was then under-secretary of state at the Home Office. Ms Flint also expressed concern and asked to be kept informed of the outcome.

It was decided that we should appeal, and to this end I was able to get advice from a local solicitor and from a solicitor friend of the treasurer of One25. Carmen added the following note in support of her claim for compensation:

> I would like to request a review of the decision due to the mental and emotional scars the rape has left me with. I am no less of a human being or woman than anyone else because I have a criminal record which was not an issue at the time. I had not offended for five years previous to the attack. I suffered an attack that almost killed me, it is something that I will have to live with for the rest of my life.

After some months delay Carmen received the outcome of the review of her application for compensation. The CICA determined that after reviewing medical reports and information obtained from the police and One25, Carmen would be compensated with the sum of £5,500. This sum was exactly half the compensation which could be expected by a person without previous criminal convictions. But it was still a victory, of sorts. Carmen accepted the award and immediately handed over £500 to One25 in thanks for the help she had received over the years. The remaining £5,000 certainly helped Carmen later on.

Carmen came through The Well and came off drugs. She left The Well and moved on to her own flat. She went on to volunteer in a charity project, and slowly managed to achieve stability in her life, staying off drugs. Last time I saw her, she was in a relationship, had a child, and was looking after that child.

Going to court gave her strength – the police really supported her, they were behind her 100 per cent. They had also saved her life, of course – finding her in the car park. They saw her through. In court, she was believed – her offender was convicted and sentenced, and that was immensely empowering. What a thing, to live through a kidnap and attempted murder, and recover from that. What a hard, hard childhood she'd had as well. What strength, to come through all that, and to set your life on an even footing.

I was so angry with the CICA people and I was also angry with the solicitors in Bristol who wouldn't represent Carmen because of those past convictions. I had been asked again to become a trustee of One25 in 2003, and had this time accepted. I think I spoke about Carmen's predicament at one of our meetings. We had a lovely treasurer at the time, who knew lots of people in law. She said, 'I've got a friend who will take this on for you,' and that's how Carmen got some compensation after all.

Of course, we initially said no to the £500, but Carmen firmly wanted to give that to One25, who had supported her over many years. She wanted other women to be able to have the chance she had been offered – that lifeline of a safe, caring home, from where real change was at last possible.

16

Black Clouds, Green Hills, Gold Standards

One of the joys for me of working with the women at The Well was earning their trust and taking them out for coffee and cake. On these occasions they sometimes shared deeply about their early lives in ways that most of us 'respectable' people rarely do.

During one of these conversations, it became evident to me that some of the residents and women I was working with had perhaps never had the opportunity to go for walks in the countryside and breathe the fresh air. Given how much the wild spaces of nature build me up and nourish me, I could not let this rest!

At One25, I had already seen the good it did our women and families to go out on trips and excursions. So we hatched a plan. It was agreed with the manager of The Well that Cliff and I, together with a member of staff, would take a group of women to the Quantock Hills for a picnic lunch and walk. We had two cars, four residents and an enormous picnic when we set off from Easton on a fine June morning in 2004. We parked at a high point, Dead Woman's Ditch on the Quantocks, and set off at a brisk pace for our picnic spot.

We soon split naturally into two groups – one slightly faster group in front with me, and the other group behind us with Cliff and the member of staff. We had not walked far, maybe a mile or so, when one of the residents suddenly started to panic. We were on a hillside, looking towards Weston-super-Mare, and there was a dark rain cloud hanging in the sky in the distance. This woman had never seen a raincloud like this before, and she was frightened by it.

At the same time, in Cliff's little group, one of the women started panicking because she had seen our group in front of her disappear over the side of the hill and out of sight!

We had to regroup quickly and calm things down. We explained to the women about perspective, the shape of rain clouds, how a slope could obscure people even though they were still quite close. We emphasized that we would not abandon them on the hills. We took the opportunity to stay together for a few minutes, getting out our flask of coffee and a snack.

It was clear that the women had no understanding of being out in the wild places, where they were not surrounded by buildings and familiar streets. They were out of their comfort zone and felt vulnerable. All their insecurities came to the surface, and this was something I had not foreseen. I had learned over the years to be comfortable in their surroundings, but they had not had the opportunity to be comfortable in mine.

We modified our pace a little, and continued on our walk together, pointing out Hinckley Point power station to our right, and Minehead to our left, until we came to our picnic spot. It was a beautiful place to share food, and we were blessed by a skylark, something none of them had seen before. We relaxed and laughed together as we ate.

The best bit of the walk came in the afternoon, as we dipped into the valley of Holford Glen to have a cream tea in a rather posh hotel. Because it was such a lovely day, we sat outside in the garden, where the women kicked off their shoes and dabbled their feet in the stream that runs through the grounds of the hotel. They were completely relaxed, and thoroughly enjoyed the cream tea, which was very generous with its cream and jam. For Lisa, one of the women, it happened to be her birthday that day, so we made a bit of a celebration – perfect timing.

The women then lay out on the grass, soaking up the sun before the final part of the walk.

However, the indulgent cream tea appeared to have been too much for two of the women, and they informed us there was no way they could get up and walk any further!

We agreed that Cliff and the member of staff, together with the two fittest women, would continue the walk to get the cars, while I remained in the hotel garden with the two other women, waiting to be picked up.

For those who went on foot, the last part of the walk involved a very steep, 45° muddy slope, followed by a demanding ascent up and over two hills, through an Iron Age fort, and back to the cars!

I stayed in the garden with the two remaining women, where we drank more tea and chatted until Cliff returned in our car, together with the worker in her car, and picked us up to drive home to Bristol.

It was a brilliant but exhausting day out, and the women talked about it for a long time afterward. Lisa in particular – who had been in Cliff's group, walking back to the cars – had enjoyed the whole day tremendously. She loved being out in the countryside, and the feeling of getting good exercise in the fresh air.

I truly believe this was a turning point for Lisa. Following this outing, she really took hold of her life. The last I heard, she was in a stable relationship, had got married and become a mother. The Quantock Hills had played a part in changing a life that day, and in fact the whole day was quite an achievement for everyone involved.

We really strived to care for the whole person in the way that we supported the women at The Well. From matching bedlinen to advice and counselling; from cups of tea in our little garden to vigorous walks in the hills; all these things helped to open their eyes to the world around them. We could see, with many of the women, that they started to expand their horizons and sense of possibilities, to value themselves and believe in a future with hope.

A report authored by Shelter in 2004[5] identified The Well as an Innovative Project, and used it as a case study, describing in detail how we worked and what made us successful. The report stated, 'The Well does not look like a hostel. The staff believe that providing high-quality accommodation promotes immediate respect from the residents; it conveys the ethos that the project is their home, where staff provide support.'[6]

Later on, The Well was cited as a 'gold standard service' in *Working with Sex Workers: Exiting*, a report by the UK Network of Sex Work Projects, March 2008.[7]

That was a real boost to us. It was a boost for the residents too – they enjoyed knowing that they lived in a 'gold standard' residence! The report identified that this was a very caring place, which it was – our team were absolutely superb. We looked after both our paid staff and our volunteers very well, and they were extremely caring.

There was one resident in The Well who made a lasting impression on me, for a range of different reasons. We got to know Trudy through the van outreach, over a number of years. When we first met, she insisted that she was eighteen years of age. In fact, she was much younger, but we had no way of knowing this. Trudy's life seemed to be dominated by her boyfriend who, at the age of fifteen, had made a career decision to become a pimp. Trudy had a bright, attractive personality, but she also had a dependence on both heroin and crack cocaine.

Trudy never came to the drop-in at the Grosvenor Centre, so our only contact with her was through the van. On these occasions, she was always in a hurry to get something to eat and some condoms and would never really engage with us, so we were unable to build an accurate picture of her life. We did, however, liaise with Social Services concerning her welfare.

Trudy disappeared from the scene for some months and it was only when she started working again that we discovered she had been pregnant and given birth to a baby, which had been adopted by a family member.

Trudy's life continued to spiral out of control and she went to prison in Eastwood Park, but did not ask for a visit. Towards the end of her sentence, she rang and asked for help with accommodation on her release from prison. We talked on the telephone and during a visit I made to her, she agreed to come to The Well. During her time in Eastwood Park, Trudy had detoxed from drugs, and she wanted to make a fresh start. At the end of her sentence, I collected her from prison and took her direct to The Well, where all went smoothly initially. She felt safe and cared for.

I cannot be sure if Trudy contacted her former boyfriend, or if he came looking for her. The result, though, was that one night she climbed over the back wall of The Well, which was 12ft high, and used drugs. Some hours later she then attempted to climb back in, but fell and broke her arm. All this activity was recorded on our CCTV and Trudy was duly challenged the following morning regarding her actions which, ludicrously, she denied.

Trudy tested positive for drug use, and when we discussed the future with her, she was unwilling to commit to living drug-free. She was therefore evicted – but not before she had been taken to hospital for treatment on her broken arm. The staff in The Well were very sad, but it was felt that this was the right decision, not least to keep the remaining residents safe.

Some months went by before our next contact with Trudy. I was driving the van back to our parking place one night, around 1 a.m., when Trudy ran out in front of the van. She was pleased to see me, and asked if I would pick her up the following day to take her to hospital, as she thought she might be pregnant. We arranged a time and an address where I could pick her up, then I left her and went home.

The following day, I drove to the address Trudy had given me and was surprised to see that all the windows and door were boarded up. I parked the car and walked to the front door to read a notice pinned there. The notice said that the house had an Anti-Social Behaviour Order (ASBO) placed on it due to drug dealing and that anyone found there would be arrested.

I walked around the front of the house and found that the boarding over one of the two downstairs windows was loose. I could hear voices inside the house, so I pulled it open a little and called Trudy's name. No one answered and the voices stopped. I kept calling for a minute or so and then, pulling the boarding open some more, I saw that it would be possible to climb up onto the window ledge and get into the house. So that's what I did.

I climbed onto the window ledge and straddled it, ready to drop into the downstairs room. It was at this point – when I had one leg inside the house, and the other outside, still holding onto the loosened boarding with my hand, that two police officers appeared and asked me what I was doing.

The officers said they had watched me read the ASBO notice on the door and then try to gain entrance to the property. Still sitting astride the windowsill, I replied that I was looking for someone, to take them to hospital. They asked for the name of this person, but I couldn't give a name. These were regular police officers – not my contacts in the vice liaison office – Trudy's identity and situation were confidential. So I refused to give a name, and they told me to get down and to accompany them to the police station, where I received a caution for entering a property with a clear ASBO notice on it.

When we were done at the police station, I returned to the property. I still needed to find Trudy. Once again, I lifted the boarding and called for her. A young man came to the window and said that Trudy had left earlier in the day. He apologized for not coming when I had called earlier, but said that they knew that the house was being watched by the police. He gave me the address of where he thought she would be.

I went to this new address, and clearly it was another crack house. This time there was no ASBO notice on the door and all the windows had been smashed, so I just called out Trudy's name. After a couple of minutes she appeared, but was only wearing a towel wrapped around her. I admit to being more than slightly impatient with her at this point, but I went off to a charity shop to get her some clothing, in order that we could go to the hospital. All this took quite a lot of time, and I was not best pleased with her.

The midwives in the hospital were brilliant and examined Trudy. She was in fact seven months pregnant. The hospital gave her good advice about getting a methadone prescription for her drug addiction, and made an appointment the following morning for her to pick this up. I took her to a hostel for the night, and arranged to pick her up the next morning.

Having left Trudy at the hostel, I then looked for my mobile phone in order to ring Cliff, and say that I would be late picking him up from work. My mobile was missing. There had only been Trudy and me in the car and together at the hospital, and I realized that she must have stolen it. I was both disappointed and cross.

The following morning, as agreed, I picked Trudy up at the hostel to take her to her appointment. She looked really unwell and asked me to buy her coffee and something to eat. I refused, saying that I was disappointed that she had stolen my phone. She denied that she had done this, and said that it was horrid and unkind of me.

I felt really bad, but I stuck to my guns, refusing to buy coffee and food. Some minutes passed before she admitted that she had stolen the mobile and had sold it to a dealer for £10 in order to buy drugs. She wasn't necessarily remorseful, but she confessed and apologized. We talked about the need for mutual trust and respect, and I bought her the coffee and food that she needed – though some of the need was probably the craving for sweet things which heroin use often brings. I hoped she had learned some kind of lesson.

I saw Trudy briefly several times over the following two weeks until one Sunday afternoon, I received a telephone call from

Trudy's mum, a lovely woman I had met a couple of months previously. Trudy had telephoned her mum from hospital telling her that she had given birth that afternoon to a baby daughter. She asked her mum to ring me requesting a visit, and please could I take in some clothing for the baby and herself.

I duly made another visit to a charity shop and bought some lovely new-born baby clothes and some clothing for Trudy. Both mother and baby were well, although the baby, of course, needed treatment for drug withdrawal. The story of the baby's birth, however, was quite shocking.

Trudy had not stayed long at the hostel where I'd dropped her off those couple of weeks ago. She had, instead, been living in a crack house and continuing to sell sex in order to buy drugs. During the Saturday night/Sunday morning before she had given birth, Trudy had smoked a lot of both heroin and crack cocaine. She had crashed out on a sofa in the crack house and had woken up late Sunday morning because of stomach pains.

The pain was acute, but Trudy did not realize that she was in labour and therefore called a taxi to take her to the Bristol Royal Infirmary. She paid her fare and got out of the taxi. But she didn't get any further. There, on the pavement outside the hospital, on a busy Sunday afternoon, Trudy gave birth to her baby. No one came to her assistance until after the birth, when she was lying on the ground, holding her new-born child, calling for someone to get help.

Trudy was taken into the Bristol Royal Infirmary, and then transferred to Southmead Hospital, where there is a birth centre and obstetric unit. This is where I visited her.

Initially, Trudy seemed committed to caring for her daughter, and was encouraged by the hospital staff to have no contact with her boyfriend. I visited several times over those first ten days or so, and we talked about her future with the baby. Social Services were, of course, involved, but Trudy showed every sign of loving and caring for the child. Trudy asked if I would take some photographs of her with the baby. I told her that my husband, Cliff, was a good photographer and she asked if he would come to the hospital and take the photos.

Cliff agreed and he and I went in together for the photoshoot. Trudy looked radiant. She was beautifully made up and looked well, having put on a little weight during her hospital stay. Cliff took some photographs of Trudy and her baby daughter and quickly made copies for her to keep. She was delighted with them, chatting with us about what a lovely memory they would make. It was as she was chatting, though, that I learned that her boyfriend/pimp had made contact, and wanted her to leave the hospital to be with him. I tried to advise her that this would be very bad news for her and the baby.

However, the following day, when I went to the ward again, I was told by the staff that shortly after our previous visit, once Cliff and I had gone, Trudy had left, with the boyfriend, leaving her baby behind in the hospital cot.

I was devastated.

I think it was about a year later that I received the tragic news of Trudy's death. She had died from a drug overdose, aged 32. Her funeral was packed, and Trudy's brave, feisty mum spoke with love and compassion about Trudy's life. She talked about her potential, her beauty and her bubbliness, but she also spoke truthfully about the choices Trudy had decided to make. It was incredibly moving, and immensely sad.

Trudy was a young woman who really messed up my emotions. I loved her courage and her ability to keep on keeping on, but I felt great pain at her inability to make good choices – choices that would have given her life and not led to death.

You can never force someone to make good choices, you can only pray and strive to make those choices available to them, always holding open the door as best you can. Through all the chaos and madness, the ups and downs we had with Trudy, I held on to the hope of change for her, right until those last few days in hospital with her baby. I lost that hope when she chose to abandon her baby, and self-medicate on heroin and crack cocaine to deal with the pain and shame.

The one redeeming end to this story is that the same family relative who had adopted Trudy's first child also adopted her daughter, and both these children are in a safe, loving home. I praise God for that.

17

A Good Pathway

Father Richard McKay's vision for safe and supported housing for male ex-offenders became a reality almost at the same time as The Well. Once again with support from Alabaré Christian Care Centres and financial help from Mr Murray, the first home for male ex-offenders – Lazarus House – was founded in 2003.

This was very timely, in that Bristol City Council had just identified in a Supporting People Strategy the city's lack of stable, long-term accommodation with wrap-around support for ex-prisoners. The strategy also stated that there was a need to move towards higher levels of support for those with complex needs, and increase the options for supported housing. So we were knocking on an opening door.

A house was identified in a quiet residential street to accommodate five male ex-offenders. These men would be referred by the Prison Service, Probation Service or another agency. The house would have twenty-four-hour staffing, with sleepover cover and random drug/alcohol testing to ensure residents and staff were safe. A full rehabilitation programme was put in place and a staff team was recruited under the excellent management of Pat Harrison.

As with previous projects, once there was something in place, and someone managing it, it was not difficult to find volunteers to help out. I remember a church group on the outskirts of Bristol who heard a talk I gave about The Well and Lazarus House. They were enthusiastic and wanted to help.

We looked at what they could offer and at what was needed, and ended up with a wonderful scheme of meal preparation which lasted for several years. A group of women would come once a week with the ingredients for a meal, and they would prepare the food together with those residents who wished to join them. Many of these men had been in prison for a long period of their lives (indeed, our first resident was a lifer who had been in prison for many years) so they had very little in the way of cooking skills. This brilliant match of need and offer worked very well, and meant a great deal to both groups of people.

It quickly became apparent that move-on accommodation was needed for residents who had completed their initial rehabilitation programme at Lazarus House and were ready for the next step. A second house in the same street became available for renting and Andrew House was founded. This house was not staffed, as it was for residents who wanted to take more personal responsibility – and they were supported from Lazarus House two doors away as needed. Residents were also encouraged to have some contact with family members, including children, though this was carefully managed and monitored.

Sometime later, a third house in the same street became available. Thomas House was the third stage in move-on accommodation and was the final one before independent living. Each stage gave more individual responsibility to residents in preparation for a fully independent life, but support was on hand whenever it was needed. The men were also, at this stage, encouraged to seek voluntary or paid employment, and many did so, and found rewarding positions which gave them a sense of worth and usefulness.

Several years later a fourth house was rented, in another area of the city. This was a three-bedroom house for residents considered ready for independent living. There was a close link with a local church, and two residents took the decision to be baptized while living there. One of the ex-residents from this fourth house went to work for two months with homeless people in a Christian hostel in Johannesburg, and upon his return to the UK visited Lazarus House to encourage residents there about his journey.

It was incredible, and so heart-warming to see the slow, steady progression of these men, who were genuinely looked after in a way that helped them make change towards an independent, fruitful and fulfilling life. Had they been left alone to make their own way after prison, many of them would have simply fallen back into the familiar ways and relationships they had known before, generally involving some kind of criminal activity, drugs or alcohol. What a privilege to be part of creating the environment where they could change, and where they could meet God.

John came to Lazarus House after spending many years in prison. On the first occasion that I met him there, shortly after his release, he invited me to see his room, of which he was clearly very proud. The room was neat and tidy, with his duvet rolled up at the foot of his bed and everything in its place. Then I glanced up and saw a girlie picture on the wall. He was instantly embarrassed and apologized to me. I remember assuring him that this was his home and I wanted him to feel that it was his.

Some years later, I was queueing outside what was the Colston Hall, now the Bristol Beacon, to go to a concert. John, accompanied by a woman, approached me and said hello. He introduced the woman to me as his partner, and told me that life was good for him now. As well as being in a long-term relationship, he had a job working for a charity. He looked happy and well, and I was delighted to meet him again.

Another couple of years later, I was looking around a local charity shop which sold furniture, and who was there but John. Having worked there during his time in supported housing, he had since been promoted to manager of the store. What a wonderful result! John was happy and healthy, and told me his life continued to go very well.

I thanked God for this beautiful transformation. People like John deserve a life with hope and a future, not one that leads to enslavement to alcohol and drugs. God is the one who transforms, but we can have a hand in creating the circumstances where the person is able to say yes to God, and opt into that transformation. What a privilege to be part of that.

What we achieved through setting up these four homes for male ex-offenders was a care pathway, which is absolutely essential for both men and women seeking to make positive changes to their lives. How can any of us achieve a dramatic life change without a safe roof over our heads and people to care for us? This is what we were seeing at The Well too – women able to change, because they were given enough support to make the positive decisions they were capable of – and to sustain those decisions. This was the pathway I had dreamed of for some years, and I felt it was the most effective way to support people for lasting change.

I still yearned for a similar home where we could accommodate women with their babies. Having a child was such a pivotal point in many of these women's lives, and such a vulnerable one. I had prayed for this for five years, and continued to do so.

In August 2004 I was invited to take part in an International Consultation on Ministry to Women in Prostitution. This took place in Wisconsin, USA, and was organized by the American Baptist Historical Society. The keynote speakers were Philip Yancey and Dr Elaine Storkey. I led a seminar entitled, 'Forming an exit strategy when women want to leave prostitution'.

The focus of my seminar was on providing a care pathway, by means of safe accommodation with wrap-around support, and to help women become aware of alternatives to their lives if they desired change. I argued that accommodation should be drug/alcohol free, with specialist help to enable residents to recover from abuse suffered throughout their lives. It is not possible to consider change from a place of abuse, or from the craziness of the streets. Our aim was to empower women to rebuild their lives through support and skills training.

The seminar attracted a lot of interest and was attended by workers from projects around the world, who said they wished they could send the women they worked with to The Well in the UK!

Back in Bristol, I had a wonderful friendship with Sister Ann Teresa, an inspirational Catholic nun who took a great interest in our work, and had a heart for vulnerable women. Sister Ann Teresa and I both, independently, read an article in

The Observer one Sunday written by Lord Hylton, a heredi-tary peer who was interested in many social issues, including housing, poverty and disability rights.

In this article, Lord Hylton expressed some opinions on the issue of prostitution in the UK. Sister Ann Teresa rang me the following day and pointed out several things in the article which she didn't fully agree with. I also had noticed these – though we were also both very pleased to read a thoughtful, kind article attempting to wrestle with the realities of a com-plex and harmful situation. We agreed that we would each write to Lord Hylton, pointing out that while we welcomed his article, there were several inconsistencies in it. And so we did.

Within days, Lord Hylton replied, with an apology, and invited us both to have lunch with him in the House of Lords! We readily accepted and were graciously treated to an enjoy-able lunch during which we were able to talk with him about our experience of working with female sex workers. Lunch was followed by a brief tour of the Houses of Parliament. It was an interesting and pleasant experience and one I remem-ber well.

Following our lunch with Lord Hylton, I wrote another letter thanking him for lunch and inviting him to come to Bristol to see One25, The Well and Lazarus House, and to meet some of the residents. Once again, Lord Hylton replied within days, ringing me at home and saying that he could come later in the same week. He said that he could drive to Bristol on his way to see family.

I was slightly alarmed at the thought of him arriving at One25, on Grosvenor Road in inner-city Bristol in an expen-sive car and suggested that if he had a 'downmarket' vehicle, it might be as well to use that one. He laughed and said that he would drive his old Škoda.

On the day of his visit, I went to our next-door neighbours on Grosvenor Road to ask our friends in the taxi company if they would kindly leave a space free, as I had an important guest visiting – a Lord from the Houses of Parliament. I then waited outside the Grosvenor Centre so that I could welcome our guest when he arrived.

And sure enough, on the dot of 6 p.m. on a warm summer Thursday evening, a bright blue Škoda appeared in Grosvenor Road. Our next-door neighbours had indeed left space for Lord Hylton to park, and several of them took charge of guiding him into the space. It was very amusing to watch this procedure, complete with lots of arm waving and shouted directions. When we were inside the Grosvenor Centre, Lord Hylton commented on the kindness of our neighbours and the strong smell of cannabis in the air! A good start to our evening together.

I gave Lord Hylton a guided tour of One25, and he was most interested to hear about the work carried out there. One thing that really drew his attention was the sight of the white plastic storage boxes high on a shelf in the drop-in area, each with a woman's name clearly showing. I explained that these contained the belongings of women who had no safe accommodation of their own. He was clearly moved to think that all of a person's precious belongings could fit into one storage box.

We also showed Lord Hylton our van, and explained how it was used for outreach, and we then moved on to The Well, which was only a short drive away. The five women then resident at The Well had each bought a cake for Lord Hylton's visit, and the table in the kitchen was laid for tea. Once again, he was very interested in the programme and asked lots of questions of both the residents and the staff while consuming vast quantities of cake and tea.

The atmosphere was relaxed and jolly – so much so that it almost became boisterous. One of the residents, noting Lord Hylton's long white beard, asked him if he had left his red coat and hat at home. He smiled and took this as harmless teasing, but I could tell that resident was struggling slightly with the dynamic of all this attention on our visitor. She wasn't someone who always knew where to draw the line – so I watched her carefully. However, the rest of the conversation passed off peacefully!

Finally, I drove Lord Hylton to Lazarus House, where the reception was very different. The five resident men had gathered in the sitting room and were all very polite, quiet and even sombre in their welcome. More tea was consumed and gradually the residents opened up as Lord Hylton asked gentle questions about their lives. He was a good listener, and was clearly moved as they told him their stories, particularly those of broken families and the loss of children because of their behaviour.

In all, Lord Hylton spent two and a half hours across our three Bristol projects. As I drove him back to Grosvenor Road to pick up his car, he said that he had been impressed with all that he had seen, and had felt particularly privileged to talk to the residents at The Well and Lazarus House. It was certainly a privilege for us to receive a visit from someone so well-informed, interested and humble.

18

Beautiful Baby

It was exciting to show Lord Hylton something of the pathway to recovery for the men and women who were resident with us at that time. This care pathway was something God had laid strongly on my heart. Also on my heart was the need for a mother-and-baby unit for female sex workers committed to change.

As well as praying about this over the years, I had tentatively pushed at some doors, and made some useful contacts. But I knew better than to press ahead with action before I was clear that God was leading me.

I did know already what this unit would be called, when it finally came to fruition – Naomi House. 'Where you go I will go, and where you stay I will stay' is what Ruth says to Naomi in Ruth 1:16 in the Bible, and I longed for somewhere where mother and baby could be together, and be supported in continuing to be together as they moved on in life.

I had developed a strong mutual friendship with a woman called Di Goodwillie, the specialist drug social worker in St Michael's Hospital. She and I had worked together over the years as we both tried to support pregnant, drug-abusing sex workers at One25. Di had years of experience dealing with pregnant sex workers, and agreed to be part of a working group to plan for and set up Naomi House.

Di had a sound understanding of Social Services, and she also understood the values and ways of working of One25. In addition, she appreciated my particular style of operating, and caught my vision. She had a very unusual ability to see lots of sides to a situation, and was therefore an extremely good person to liaise between different services.

Di's manager, Chrissy Savage, also agreed to be a member of this working group. Both women brought an enormous amount of expertise and commitment towards making Naomi House a reality. The vice liaison officer in Avon and Somerset Police was also supportive and enthusiastic.

We had a working group. Now we needed a business plan. We discussed together what we wanted to provide, how we wanted to work, and what the house would achieve. Then I got to work writing the plan.

The object of Naomi House would be to provide safe housing for mothers and babies where drug misuse and risk from sex work had been a problem. It would be only for women who were motivated to change their lifestyle for the benefit of their babies and themselves. Similar to The Well, the support offered at the house would help them develop personal and life skills, giving hope for the future, and opening up the opportunity to move towards sustained, independent lives for the women with their children. The house would come under the auspices of One25, and be overseen by their management board, providing continuity for those women who were already accessing services through the drop-in or van outreach. Crucially, it would provide a realistic alternative to children being removed from their mothers.

The difficulties faced by pregnant, drug-abusing female sex workers are complex and multiple. For Social Services and NHS Maternity Services, these issues pose an enormous problem as they seek to support mother and baby, and take decisions for the benefit of them both. Each of these services expressed strong support for a concept like Naomi House, which would bring together the multiple requirements for a woman wishing to create a life where she could safely care for her baby.

In order to have a chance of looking after a baby properly, a pregnant, drug-using woman would have to cease chaotic drug use – a massive ask to start with. She would need to get a prescription alternative drug (usually methadone), find and furnish accommodation, register with a doctor and with a midwife specializing in pregnancies with drug addiction, and keep all her medical appointments. She would need to sort out benefits, and learn the skills necessary for managing money and a home. For many women, this would have to be done without any support from a reliable family network.

In 2007, of the ninety-seven mothers and pregnant women One25 worked with, fifty-two had their children removed into care. To emphasise the complexity of the situation, and the adversity faced by many of these women, I included in my business plan two case studies of women we knew through One25, whose lives we felt could be transformed by a service like Naomi House.

Case Study No. 1
Sally spent her childhood in care, she is now a substance user and she has absolutely no family support. She was homeless, sex work-ing and seven months pregnant when One25 started working

with her. Her baby was born and went straight into drug withdrawal. Sally stayed with her baby throughout the three-week withdrawal process in hospital. It is acknowledged that the first four weeks of a baby's life are a significant time for bonding. The baby went immediately into care after withdrawing. Sally was determined to get her baby back, so she managed to get a flat; she got on a methadone prescription and started to access services. Sally and her baby were reunited after two months' separation.

Due to Sally's change of lifestyle and choices, she had disassociated from all her old friends and contacts. This inevitably left her very lonely and isolated, intensified by her lack of family support. Daytimes were slightly easier as she accessed services and became dependent on these in the process. However, evenings were problematic because of her loneliness and isolation. She applied to go to a mother-and-baby rehabilitation unit in Cornwall, but sadly she only lasted three weeks there because she was too far away from the services she had become dependent on. Her baby was removed again and she is currently living back in Bristol. Naomi House would be ideal for Sally and her baby.

Case Study No. 2

Hayley is a pregnant 35-year-old lady. Her childhood was spent in care and she has had no positive parenting or role models whatsoever. She has four children, all of whom are already in care. Due to Hayley's history with Social Services, they would automatically be involved with her new baby. When the baby is born it would go straight into drug withdrawal and Hayley would be allowed to stay with the baby during this five to ten-day process. The baby would then go directly into foster care while court proceedings begin, and Hayley would return to her hostel accommodation.

One of the primary issues is Hayley's lack of stable accommodation. The hostel is not dry (substance use is permitted) and is therefore a very vulnerable place for Hayley as she attempts to make lifestyle changes. There is a lack of appropriate services for her to access. In Bristol, the only mother-and-baby unit is available to under 25 year olds, thus disqualifying Hayley from this specialist support which she so desperately needs.

The hostel mentioned was not for mothers with alcohol- or drug-addiction issues. Indeed, at the time, there were only three residential rehabilitation centres in the UK for mothers with addiction problems, and none of these were specifically for women wishing to exit sex work. It was not easy to get into one of these centres, and they were all far from Bristol. The only alternative was being allocated general housing locally, which was often unsuitable, potentially harmful, and often led to relapse and the removal of the baby.

I finished the business plan, and on the basis of that, we consulted, many times, with many people and organizations. We prayed, we had meetings, we fundraised, we held talks, we spoke to churches. Bit by bit, we refined our vision, clarified our expectations and built up support. This happened over a number of years. It was an extraordinary effort by many people – clearly showing the enormous commitment to and the huge need for somewhere like Naomi House.

Through a contact in Bristol Christian Fellowship, a couple, Robin and Di Self, came forward and offered a house to rent which they owned and was alongside their own home. It was a three-bed house with a large downstairs kitchen and three other rooms, which had the potential to be developed into office space and a fourth bedroom. There was a large upstairs bathroom that could be for the use of the four residents, and there was space for an additional shower room and toilet to be put in for staff use. To the rear of the property was a large garden with an open outlook – I knew how treasured a garden space would be. The house was in a safe residential area, well away from the inner city. It was perfect. God had provided.

Policies and safeguarding had to be agreed with Social Services, incorporating advice from other providers of residential accommodation. Alterations had to be made by the builders, and of course, bullet-proof glass was fitted to all downstairs windows and doors. It took a lot of work, but at last, we were in a position to advertise for staff.

This time, we were looking after not only vulnerable women, but also their babies. It was agreed that Naomi House would have twenty-four-hour staffing, with sleepover on night shifts, but we soon changed this to have a member of staff who was awake and working through the night, as a further safeguarding measure. We found a wonderful manager for the house – a trained and experienced social worker, Eve, who was also a Christian, with a big heart as well as solid professional expertise. Eve would manage the staff we recruited, and she would put a training programme in place for them, as well as a programme of support for the residents, which included multi-agency involvement.

Each of the residents' rooms was beautifully furnished, with matching colour-coded curtains, bedding and towels. Each had a single bed, a cot for the baby, a wardrobe and a chest of drawers. Also provided were small tabletop refrigerators in which mothers could keep food and baby milk. These were the gift of a small group of mothers in Christ Church, a church in Clifton, who also provided a dressing gown and pyjamas for each resident.

The shared sitting room was homely and comfortable, and would become well-used by the residents. All the furniture was the generous gift of Park Furnishers in Bristol, who allowed Di Goodwillie to select whatever items she thought appropriate. The furniture and carpets were a truly generous gift and the result of just a five-minute talk I gave one Sunday evening to a small group of people in Christ Church, Clifton. You just can't tell what will come of each little step you take!

The kitchen was big enough to have a large pine table which seated eight people comfortably, together with a freezer and separate refrigerator and two electric cookers. The office for staff was situated just inside the front door of the house, in order to monitor comings and goings. Both front and back entrances were alarmed, making the house safe.

Admissions were recommended as early as possible in a woman's pregnancy – ideally before thirty weeks – as this would allow time for the women to engage with relevant services, and have all their assessments completed well before the birth of their baby. Each resident had an allocated social worker who carried out an in-depth assessment within the first month of admission and would attend all reviews, liaising closely with Naomi House staff throughout the placement.

Naomi House opened in 2008 with its first resident. And our first resident deserves her own story!

It just so happened that I was the team leader on the One25 van the night before Naomi House was due to open. We were flagged down by a woman in one of our usual areas and she got on the van. I was in the driver's seat when I heard this very excited woman claiming that she was going into Naomi

House the following morning, and that this would be her tenth baby. I sneaked a look into the back of the van and, sure enough, there was Rita – heavily pregnant, and full of bright confidence that this would be the baby she would be able to keep – the other nine having been taken into care.

Rita duly arrived as Naomi House's first resident the next day. She had the pale-green room, which looked out over the back garden, and she developed a love of watching the birds from her window. She actually gave birth in the house a few weeks after arriving. The staff had taken her to Southmead Hospital because she thought she was in labour, but the midwife there had sent her home again. Within an hour of returning to Naomi House, she gave birth to a healthy baby girl!

Rita had already expressed her commitment to a new way of life, and she worked hard at addressing the issues that had resulted in her drug addiction and sex working. Other residents looked up to her and saw her as something of a role model. She was able to live in Naomi House under Housing Benefit for around eighteen months before moving on to independent living, while still being supported by staff. She was very realistic about the move towards independence, and took steps to ensure she wasn't tempted back into old ways and old relationships.

To my knowledge, Rita still has her daughter with her, and she was allowed, through Social Services, to make contact with another of her daughters.

Rita's was a precious, precious story that showed what a huge difference the care received in Naomi House made. After all those babies she had been unable to look after, she was able to turn things around, thanks greatly to the provision of accommodation, the care of the staff, the structured involvement of all the relevant agencies and the willingness of all involved to give her the time she needed to be ready to move on with the next step.

Much of the day-to-day funding for Naomi House staff was covered by Bristol City Council through Housing Benefit, and they had taken the decision to allow residents to remain in the house for up to twenty-three months – even though it was a more expensive option than other housing. This was crucial. There is never a quick fix, and I have seen so many people receive some care but not enough and not for long enough, meaning that they cannot sustain the progress they make.

One of the rules of Naomi House was that residents had to agree to being 'buddied' whenever they left the building to go to shops, medical appointments, or any other meeting. This was to ensure their safety. As individual residents progressed in their time and understanding of the issues which had resulted in prostitution and substance abuse, buddying became less and less until it was no longer needed.

Once again, Naomi House was drug- and alcohol-free – even more important, in my opinion, where there are children involved. Residents were randomly tested for drugs and alcohol. This was in fact something which the residents themselves valued, as they took pride in being clean of drugs.

It was wonderful to see lives transformed and residents flourish and take a pride in themselves and their babies. Their appearances changed, together with their outlook on a future life with their child. One resident who had always worn dark clothing and was reluctant to have eye contact had a personality makeover! She started wearing colourful clothing and caring about her body and appearance. She even took up kick boxing! These women now had hope in a future – something most of them had not experienced for years.

One resident of Naomi House had a particularly harrowing experience just hours before she was due to arrive with us. In June 2009 Jenny was kidnapped from the street, the day before she was expected at the house, and was raped five times by her kidnapper and his friend. She was then dumped on the street early in the morning and made her way to One25, waiting for a member of staff to arrive.

Thankfully, the first person to arrive that morning was Jenny's caseworker, who immediately responded to her situation. The vice liaison officer at Trinity Road Police Station was informed, and Jenny was taken for the necessary medical examinations. She was extremely traumatized and needed a lot of support, especially with the process of reporting the rape to the police.

Jenny came to Naomi House later that day, where the staff team and other residents began to give her the love and care she needed to help her recovery. During the years I had known Jenny working on the streets, she had been emotionally closed down and difficult to engage with. With unconditional and tough love, and with specialist help appropriate to her needs, Jenny began slowly to engage with the staff, and we could see positive changes in her. She was transformed into a beautiful woman with a smile that would light up any room.

Jenny's baby was born in September 2009 – a beautiful girl – but also traumatized. With ongoing love and support, though, Jenny's daughter flourished, meeting all her developmental stages. Jenny stayed resolutely drug-free, and mother and daughter had a strong maternal-infant attachment. I remember Jenny used to enjoy taking her baby to the local park, and also loved going along to a weekly church coffee morning nearby for a cuppa and a chat.

Had Jenny not already been assessed for a place in Naomi House, a place of safety and help during this late stage of pregnancy, I believe this story would have ended very differently. Having no home of her own and no support, she would have self-medicated with heroin and lost the opportunity to keep her much-wanted baby – a scenario I had witnessed many, many times.

After her stay at Naomi House, Jenny and her daughter successfully moved away from Bristol. The rapists were brought to trial and Jenny courageously gave evidence in the Crown Court over two days. Both were found guilty on all charges and received hefty prison sentences. Jenny's was a wonderful story of restoration, justice and mercy.

Not every woman who came to Naomi House, in the three years it was open, was able to maintain a lifestyle in which she could build a new life for herself and her baby. However, the intensive support provided there did make an enormous difference to women's lives.

Indeed, in just the first fifteen months of opening, we saw these results:

- Nine mothers, along with their babies or toddlers, were supported for an average stay of six to twelve months, and were offered ongoing support when they moved on.
- All nine mothers accessed the therapeutic and skills programmes, and saw improvements in their health, self-care, self-esteem, addiction issues, parenting and life skills, and emotional wellbeing.

- All nine women remained abstinent from illegal drug use. In addition, five also became abstinent from prescribed heroin substitutes, such as methadone.
- Three women relapsed temporarily, but were then supported back to stability and positive outcomes while their baby/toddler was kept safe.
- Move-on packages were implemented for three women and babies, linking with other relevant agencies and community projects, such as GPs and nurseries.
- All nine women rebuilt family links.

In 2011, three years after opening, Naomi House closed due to a change in funding. The twenty-three months of care covered by Housing Benefit was reduced by Bristol City Council to just twelve weeks. This made it virtually impossible for us to operate. How could a woman give birth to their baby, address their substance misuse, learn parenting skills, plan for the future and find a home for themselves and their child during their allotted stay of just twelve weeks? I challenge any one of us women to say we could do this. I know that I could not have done so.

Yes, Naomi House was expensive for the time women were there. However, the difference in the futures of those women was enormous, compared to where they would have been without our service. The saving over a lifetime, to health and social care, substance-misuse services, the care system, mental health services, is going to be incalculable. Investing intensively at the point of having a child makes the rest of life more likely to be healthy, safe and positive – which saves society a lot of money, as well as a lot of pain.

A couple of weeks following the closure of Naomi House, I was contacted by a Bristol magistrate who had just learned of the loss of the service. She was very disappointed that the magistrates would no longer have anywhere to refer pregnant sex workers to, and thought it was a huge loss to the city. She and many others asked me if I would consider seeking funding to open another mother-and-baby home, which was sorely needed, but this was something I no longer had the energy or heart to do.

We had prayed and planned. We had teamed up and raised funds. We had created the most wonderful, wholehearted, safe, wrap-around service for marginalized, vulnerable women and their babies. God had worked through us, and we had seen lives changed and women being saved . . . and we had been shut down.

The closure of Naomi House left me wounded, bereft, angry and even with a sense of bitterness. Had Naomi House just been a good idea of mine, but not God's project? Had God closed the door?

Once again, I took myself away – this time to Sheldon, a retreat centre in Devon, and one of my favourite places to be alone. I needed to be in the wild places again, to find myself, and to find God.

19

Nothing is Wasted:
Be Broken by Love

On the advice of my spiritual director, I took along some large pieces of paper and some coloured pens. Initially, I was far too angry and hurt to be able to get down to business with God. It took me quite a few days of simply walking on Dartmoor and breathing deeply in the raw beauty of his creation before I could even sit with him again, and take a look at the reality of Naomi House.

When I could, over the period of a day, I forced myself to write down all my negative thoughts about the closure of Naomi House on the top half of my large piece of paper – and there were many. It took me hours. I cried, and hurt, and wrote, getting all my thoughts and pain down on that paper.

Later, halfway down the sheet, I wrote in large letters, 'GOD'.

Once I had placed God at the centre of that piece of paper, slowly and after some time, I began to write down some of the positive outcomes of Naomi House. As I wrote, the positives began to grow in number and in meaning.

I wrote the names of the women who had been valued, sometimes for the first time in their lives. I wrote down all the times someone had been able to get free from the hold of drugs or alcohol. I wrote of the change in the faces of women who could start being released from the effects of abuse in their lives. I wrote the story of women learning to live away from dependence on unhealthy relationships, or on sex work as the only way to make a living.

I wrote of babies being held by their mothers, of women being able to care for their children, whom they loved. I wrote of homes and families where before there had only been chaos and separation.

I wrote of the grace of God, who always wants to meet each one of us, who always has hope, even for the most difficult and distant life. I wrote of the God who sees just one, single life as worth changing, worth giving to, worth dying for.

Slowly, and through many tears, I saw that in God, nothing is wasted. Every life touched by living in Naomi House was changed for the good. Every mother who had lived in the house had experienced loving and caring for their baby in a home where they, in turn, were loved and cared for.

For the babies, they were held and looked after by mothers who were now in their right minds – no drugs, no alcohol, no abuse. The bonding between mother and baby, which is so very vital in a child's early development, had been able to take place.

Each life had been touched by God, and that touch could never be taken away.

At last, I saw how precious Naomi House had been for each little family who lived there, and what a very precious experience it had been for all of us who were involved with it. Yes, it was gone, but the love we had shown and given away over those three years was still alive, still working, still changing people.

To this day, I grieve for the loss of Naomi House. I am still heartbroken. But somehow, I can thank God for that heartbreak, without which I never would have done the things he did through me. I was broken by his love – the love he gave me, and the love he had for all the hurting people I worked with. If I hadn't loved, I could have stayed intact, I could have had my heart remain whole. But I let his love break me, and because of that, his love flowed out to marginalized women, to their children and their families.

I thank my heavenly Father for taking me to that place, and showing me the value of Naomi House, and how his love is never wasted. I thank him also for my own healing.

The four men's homes we had set up – Lazarus, Andrew and Thomas houses, together with the move-on house – all also closed, due to lack of funding for these expensive but effective schemes. How short-sighted this is. How infuriating, and how wrong.

But nothing is ever lost.

If you have shown God's love to someone, or spoken godly words to them, that will remain. Each and every resident of those houses had the opportunity to live safely in a home where they were valued for themselves and encouraged to go deeper. Some found within themselves the courage and determination to take hold of their lives and to live without mind-altering drugs. For others, that was not their time, but we hold them before God the healer. Nothing is wasted.

You cannot ever know whether someone will change, when given the opportunity. We assessed each resident carefully before admitting them, but we still couldn't guarantee change. We could only offer the opportunity where there was a good likelihood that this person would be able to take it up.

Without the opportunity, no one can change. Jesus offered us the opportunity to change when he died for us, but only we can decide to accept his offer. Still he waits, arms open wide, heart broken, the best possibility for our future.

Would I have done anything differently with Trudy, if I'd known in advance that her story would end with death from drug use? Would I have thought, 'Well, I won't waste my time and our money on Trudy, because she isn't going to succeed'? I don't think so. I think, very fundamentally, that it is God's desire for me to love these people, however they decide to respond to his love.

Even though she died, Trudy had come face-to-face with God's love. Through One25 and The Well, she would have known – have had demonstrated to her – that she was valuable, beautiful, important and worth something. She would have known that she was loved. That in itself is an outcome. I can still say, that to the best of my ability, I gave the love of Jesus to Trudy – in a very imperfect way, of course, but without us, how would she have known that he was interested in her? That he loved her? That her struggles broke his heart?

One thing I gleaned from the residents at The Well was that here was somewhere they knew they would be welcomed and accepted for who they were, at the place they were at. They were not accepted and loved for who we wanted them to be, for where we wanted them to get to, not even for their potential. They were accepted and loved because they were worth accepting and loving, right there and then, because that's what Jesus does.

Back when I was working at One25, Sister Annaliese was approached by a young filmmaker. He was an American student doing a project on some of the social ills in the USA, and he had heard about the ministry of the Community of the Sisters of the Church in Bristol, and of One25. He travelled to Bristol and talked to one of the women working on the streets, named Veronica. He wanted Veronica to tell her story on film, and she consented. Annaliese and I were worried about this, as we were concerned that Veronica was being set up as a victim.

Veronica was addicted to both heroin and crack cocaine, as was her husband. They had one son, secondary school age, and were living in one room, sleeping on mattresses on the floor and sharing the kitchen and bathroom with a number of other people in the house.

The filmmaker spent a couple of weeks 'hanging out' with Veronica and her family. He was visibly shocked at their life-style, and often frustrated by the chaos, and the fact that he would turn up to film at an agreed time, only to find that Veronica was either missing or that she was totally out of it due to her drug use.

The young filmmaker formed a relationship of trust with Veronica and her son, and did not treat them simply as vic-tims. He got to know them and learned about their lives. Then, in the third week of filming, he arrived at Veronica's home to learn that she had been rushed to hospital, suffering from an overdose of a cocktail of drugs. Veronica did not recover. Her young son was immediately cared for by his grandmother.

And here is the crux. The young filmmaker had a choice at that time. He could have stopped all contact with Veronica's son upon her death and gone home and made his film. In-stead, he saw himself as part of the story. He kept in contact with the boy over many years. He encouraged him to study and to look to the future.

I believe he had allowed God's love to break his heart. He had allowed himself to be affected by what he had seen during his time in Bristol, and he had chosen to respond.

Veronica's son's life was also changed by the continuing interest and support from this young man who started out as a stranger but became, through his commitment, a wonderful, positive role model for someone who desperately needed that. This boy now has a hope and a future because someone chose not to resist or turn away, but to be broken by the love of God for hurting people, and to act on that.

So, will you allow yourself to be broken by love?

After the closure of Naomi House, so many people said to me, 'Come on, Val,' 'Have another go,' 'You can do it!' It was almost a pressure on me. It got to the point that I felt people were disappointed in me, but I couldn't do it. Not again. It wasn't the plan for me now.

Anyway, why was it only me they were asking?

Nothing is wasted, but still, something is needed. There are still women on the streets selling sex because they don't have the opportunity to see a different way. There are still men and women struggling with alcohol- or drug-dependency, and the associated impact on housing, health, relationships and family.

Where are the people who are going to come and help? Why aren't they saying, 'God, send me, I'm available'?

You don't have to be brilliant, or perfect, or the expert in something. I wasn't. You just need to be inspired to have a go. God will do the rest, if you rely on him and listen to him.

Where are your instincts? What are the things that make you cross, or sad, or broken-hearted – the things that feel too big for you to solve? Will you offer yourself to God, for him to involve you in some way? Will you risk it?

Do you have a choice?

God equips those he calls to do a task. Sometimes we have to come out of our comfort zone, but God is there. You aren't ever promised success or even predictability, it's much more fragile, more dependent than that – you wouldn't need a broken heart otherwise. You have to love first, in order to help, and that love will open you up to pain, and break you and heal you. But whatever you do put in, it is not wasted. You show God to people, and he remains.

20

Running Down the Hillside

I was 70 years old when Naomi House closed. I had had twenty raucous, extraordinary, rollercoaster years with God, breaking and healing as he showed me how to get alongside men and women who needed to see his love, and to see their value in his eyes. Amazingly, even when I had stopped volunteering with One25 and The Well, and Naomi House was gone, God continued to use what I had learned through this time.

In 2010 I was asked to carry out an audit of a home for trafficked women, run by a Catholic charity. Human trafficking has become the modern-day form of slavery, and in global economics is second only to drug trafficking, bigger even than the international arms trade.[8] Men and women are tricked into believing that they may have a better life with meaningful employment. Children are sold to traffickers by parents or relatives living in poverty.

There are few agencies addressing this complex and dangerous trade which is backed by coercion, fear and personal threat.

A lady I knew well had set up this charity, to work with men and women who had been trafficked. Several safe houses had been established in the UK and because of my experience,

I was invited to carry out an external audit of one of these – a home for trafficked women. In this mother-and-baby home, each resident was either pregnant or already had a child. In July 2010, I spent a week visiting the house, where I interviewed each resident, with their permission, and all members of staff and volunteers. I then made a detailed report for the trustees of my findings.

The experience was truly moving as each of the residents described how they had been trafficked, lied to, raped and they and their families threatened with violence during the process of trafficking. One of the residents was a young British woman who had been taken to Greece aged 14 and sold by her own mother to traffickers. Over a period of four years, this young woman was sold on to other traffickers until she managed to escape and made her way back to the UK. She was then 18 years of age, pregnant and had no documents of identification or any means of contacting her mother. A whole process had to be undertaken in order to re-establish her identity as a British subject. She was so deeply traumatized that she only spoke of herself in the third person, never having eye contact or appearing to show any emotion whatsoever.

The project was superb – professionally run, and meeting a desperate need. It was a privilege to spend a short time there, using my experience to identify what they were doing well, and any aspects I felt could be improved. My eyes were opened to the desperation and violence experienced by these courageous women. My heart ached as I listened to their stories.

During the time spent planning for The Well, Lazarus House and Naomi House, and then supporting staff and residents living in them, Cliff and I worshipped with Bristol Christian Fellowship. This church had closed down, and we moved on to St Matthew's Church in Cotham, in the centre of Bristol. A year or so after joining, I was asked by the curate if I would help run their toddler group, which took place in an area very close to my old patch of St Paul's.

I replied to the curate that toddlers were not really my thing, but that I would like to give it a go in the hope of establishing relationships with the parents! So began my involvement with 'Stay and Play', and this has continued for many years.

During this time, I have met and befriended some wonderful women from a range of nationalities. Many are Muslim, with a large number of Somalis. We have laughed together, and shared each other's lives. My past experience of working with people on the margins of our society has been beneficial, as I have been able to help and advise on issues to do with housing, benefits and support. It has been an enormous privilege to see these resourceful and brave women, often living quite difficult lives, but providing wonderfully for their children.

In 2019 I was asked if I would consider mentoring the manager of a women's night shelter, Val Thompson. Val worked for Crisis Centre Ministries[9] in inner-city Bristol and managed Spring of Hope, a twelve-bed shelter for vulnerable women. The space is very special and offers women safety, love, care as well as advice and emergency supplies of food and clothing.

Val and I met initially to see if we related to each other and, agreeing that we could work together, decided upon monthly meetings. I consider it a privilege to support Val in this way, talking and praying together about her work for these precious women, informed by my own experiences.

Many new friendships have, then, been made since my time with One25, The Well and Naomi House, but also, many of the women I knew then are still in my life now. I love the little surprising moments when someone pops up and shouts, 'Val! Remember me?' I always know a brilliant story is about to be told.

One such 'Remember me?' took place just before Christmas 2019. I was just leaving Marks & Spencer and feeling rather frazzled when a clear voice shouted through the crowd, 'Hi, Val, remember me?' It was Cara. She ran up to me and gave me a hug. 'I'm clean,' she said, 'and I have found God! Can't stop now, but thanks!' And she disappeared into the crowd.

I'd known Cara in my One25 days, but what a difference I could see now. Her face was glowing, her chin was up, she was no longer skin and bone like she had been. She had used to look so wrecked, and now, she was healthy and happy, with long hair in beautiful condition. With drug use, the hair is one of the first things to suffer, becoming thin, straggly, and falling out. Now here was this beautiful woman with a healthy head of gorgeous hair! When you see men and women out to score drugs, they are focused, head down, shoulders hunched, beetling along, looking for what they need. Cara was upright, poised, strong and relaxed – a woman confident in the world she is a part of.

You notice all these things in a split second, and you see a person who is thriving – and then they thank you for being a part of that transformation! What a privilege! In fact, I think Cara was out evangelizing in town that day!

On two occasions when my husband, Cliff, and I have been spending a day out in Weston-super-Mare we have had 're-member me' encounters – both times when we have been enjoying a cup of coffee in a café. As you can imagine, eyebrows were raised by other customers as the women shared honestly and without shame how their lives had been changed and they were no longer working on the streets or using drugs.

I received a call some time ago from a woman I had not seen or heard from for some years. Diana had a particularly likeable personality but during her years of 'madness' (her word) on the streets, she was hard to work with because of her chaotic drug use. Diana was very well known by the police as a prolific offender – something which makes her story all the more amazing!

Diana had a bubbly personality but rarely let her guard down, giving the impression that she was tough and resilient. In fact, her life had been incredibly sad and hard, having been sexually abused in her family home, and later in the foster home in which she was placed.

Diana had engaged with One25 during the time we had known her, but suffered extreme violence and rape shortly before disappearing from Bristol. We had no idea what had happened to her after that. How amazing to think that years later, she would want to phone up and tell One25 how her life had changed.

Because of the severity of the violence and rape perpetrated against her, Diana had needed hospital treatment, during which she was given methadone for her heroin addiction. After some weeks in hospital, in an effort to begin life afresh, she had left Bristol.

Over a period of a couple of years, Diana came off methadone. For the first time in her adult years, she was drug-free. She started volunteering with a project similar to One25, and then got a paid job with them. Her job was working with female sex workers, and she was funded partly through the NHS and partly by the police. Once a drug-addicted offender, Diana had gone full circle!

Diana was also happily married and settled with a man who knew of her past and who was kind and supportive of her during her recovery. Wow – what a story of transformation! It gives me such a lift, to hear a story like Diana's. Thank you, Lord, there's a life restored.

Remember Susan, the woman who suffered such horrific burns in Bristol? She gave her life to Jesus in my sitting room. That new home we had helped her move into some years before was a decisive moment. I'm not saying everything changed immediately, but it was a real turning point.

Initially, Susan carried on working. But on her own, not pimped. The guy who had pimped her had moved on to someone else. Because she wasn't living in the area, she wasn't steeped in the life she had previously had. Being on methadone, she wasn't consumed with the need to score. Sometimes, on methadone, people need a bit more, and they occasionally 'top up' with some heroin. For a little while, she was on her methadone prescription, and would go and work from the streets if she felt she needed to top up, or pay an electricity bill, or buy a pair of trainers. So there was a period for some years where she was still working, still on methadone, but stable and not on heroin.

Then, after that period, I heard from a mutual acquaintance that Susan wanted to get in touch with me. By this stage, I was retired. Because I was no longer associated in any way with One25, this became a friendship rather than a relationship with a support worker.

We met up from time to time, and went out for coffee. Then after a while, I started inviting her home sometimes, so we could chat in more depth. One day, we were chatting and she started asking about my faith. So I shared about Jesus, and what God meant to me.

In 2014, Justin Welby was coming to Bristol Cathedral, and I said to Susan, 'Do you want to come see the Archbishop of Canterbury?' We went along, and after the event, David, my son, was talking to the archbishop, so I went up too, and said, 'Can I introduce you to my friend Susan?' He was lovely to her, and she was absolutely chuffed to have met him.

I said to her a few weeks later, 'You know, Susan, God has a plan for your life.' I showed her Jeremiah 29[10] and I said, 'Have you got a Bible?' She didn't have a Bible, but said she would like one please.

We drove to the Christian book shop and found a Bible she liked, with large print. When we took it to the counter, she asked for one that no one else had opened or looked at. The shop assistant kindly went away and found another one, still wrapped up.

We went back to my house and had a cup of tea, and Susan asked to be prayed for. 'What for?' I asked her.

'I think I'd like to know Jesus,' she said. So I prayed a really simple prayer, and she gave her life to Jesus.

I took her home later and the next morning, early, 7 a.m. or so, the phone rang. It was Susan. She said, 'Val, I've been up all night, vomiting.'

'Are you ill?' I asked. 'Was it the cake? Something you ate? Something I gave you?'

'No, stupid,' said Susan. 'I've been vomiting out all the sh** from my life, all night.'

'Are you OK now?'

'Yes, I feel good now, because it's all gone. I want to go to church.'

I phoned the pastor of a good community church I knew and explained that Susan would like to come along. I went with her the first few times, then she settled there herself. She decided to get baptized, and they invited me to come and help with the baptism. What a privilege to stand there in the water, and baptise her into Christ.

When she had come up out of the water, Susan gave the most amazing testimony about her life. She told the congregation that she had been a prostitute and a drug addict, and that with God's help she was now free, and her life was transformed.

There was absolute silence. You could hear a pin drop. She carried on, saying she had become like a new person, and that's why she had wanted to get baptized. By the end of her testimony, there was cheering and whooping like I've never heard. It was incredibly moving, seeing her stand there, in her sopping-wet clothes, with a towel around her shoulders and a radiant face, telling everyone about God transforming her life.

Not long after that, I had a call from Susan, saying, 'Val, I've got a question.' It was a Friday. 'I've got a friend coming this evening – a man – is it OK for me to have a friend coming?'

I said, 'Is it for business?'

She said, 'Yes. I can't pay the electric bill.'

'Susan, that's not right,' I replied. 'This is a test and you need to trust God that you'll be able to pay that bill.'

'OK,' she replied. 'I'll tell him it's off.' And she cancelled it.

She somehow paid the bill, I don't know how. I once took her shopping and got her groceries when the benefits people messed up her payment, but I have not given her money. I could have given her the money for that electricity bill, but that would not have been right – it would have been me saving her out of my own strength. She had to trust God, not just me.

Susan stopped sex working altogether, and starting volunteering. She's crazy about animals, and she volunteered with an animal welfare charity. She loved it, and they loved her. It gave her confidence, being able to work. Then later on, she decided she wanted to get paid work and come off benefits.

She worked for two years as a cleaner. She started work at 6.30 a.m. and finished at 1 p.m., and walked four miles to work every day. She's gutsy. She's such a strong woman. I gave her a reference. I said I'd never worked with her, but I'd known her for a number of years, and I trusted her. After two years, she was asked if she would become a supervisor, so she now supervises other cleaners.

Susan is completely healed of drug dependency. Some people get clean of drugs, but always live with the cravings. Susan is healed from that completely. Only God can do a work like that. With enormous courage and determination, and with her faith now firmly in God, she has overcome mountains in her life. It has not been easy. It is a privilege to have her friendship and her trust.

Another encouragement arrived in the post one morning at home, in 2012 – many years after I had been One25's project manager. It was from one of the women we had worked with over a long period, and in it she shared her feelings – in her own words – about the project:

Val, let me start by saying that I love you to death and I have known you for a long time, many years. You have always made me feel accepted, beautiful and loved. At times you have, to me, took my mum's place, given me advice and such.

You created One25 many years ago and I believe you never thought it would become as big and as important as it is now.

I feel and I am sure that the staff, volunteers, and the girls feel that One25 is a family – a place that we are loved accepted and helped, just like a family should be like. You know that anybody can create a drop-in, but you have created a family for all of us. Most importantly, you have changed the way people see us. We are no longer seen as scum, we are understood and people understand that we need help to get ourselves back into society. You are responsible for this.

One25 is a living, breathing family and it loves and gives out with 125 per cent.

She was so right in thinking that I never dreamed One25 would ever become the large organization it is today, with around forty paid members of staff, many more volunteers, and even its own building. In 2005, Bristol Christian Fellowship gave the most amazingly generous gift – they signed over the Grosvenor Centre to One25. One25 now has its own property, with no strings attached and no rent to pay. My very small seed has blossomed into a big-hearted, firm-footed professional organization, which still cares for the street-based female sex workers.

It is such a blessing to see all the people continuing this valuable work. There are no quick fixes; the work is hard and long haul, but so, so precious and worthwhile. I can honestly say it was the best job I ever had, although for myself, I could never call it a job, even when I was paid for it!

As the work I founded and was involved with became more widely known, I received some awards in recognition. In 2002 I received the Member of the British Empire (MBE) award in the Queen's Birthday Honours List, and in 2018 I was awarded an Honorary Doctorate of Laws from the University of Bristol. Finally, in December 2021, I was given the Freedom of the City of Bristol. This is truly amazing – particularly as it would appear that I am the first woman in Bristol ever to receive the Freedom of the City.

I am humbled by all these honours, and each time deliberated about whether to accept them. In the end, I did accept, not to recognize any achievements by myself, but on behalf of the marginalized women I had worked with, loved and been accepted by – and on behalf of marginalized women everywhere.

There are many women with very little power or influence in the world. We can think that our way out is to gain what the world thinks power is, but actually our way out is to know the power of Jesus. That power is the power which transforms. What great power we have, when we work with him and in him.

There have been situations in my life that have caused me deep-seated pain. The pain has not gone away, and I will have questions when I meet with my Maker. I am, however, aware that God has been with me throughout the pain and enabled me to carry on. Sharing in the suffering of others is costly. It has also shaped me. I am so grateful to my heavenly Father for the healing he provided for me.

In 2019 I was asked by Peter Hill – husband of Helen Hill, who worked with me at One25 – to appear in a video, which would be part of a course he was designing called Loved+Liked. The course can be found online,[11] and is a wonderful resource, showing us how not only does God love us, but he also actually likes us, and really does take delight in who we are and how we are.

The episode I was to contribute to was entitled 'Called and Equipped', and in the video, I was asked whether there was a particular Bible passage which was important to me, or which had been my inspiration. This was not difficult for me – I chose Isaiah 58:6–12:

Is not this the kind of fasting I have chosen:
to loose the chains of injustice
and untie the cords of the yoke,
to set the oppressed free
and break every yoke?
Is it not to share your food with the hungry
and to provide the poor wanderer with shelter –
when you see the naked, to clothe them,
and not to turn away from your own flesh and blood?
Then your light will break forth like the dawn,
and your healing will quickly appear;
then your righteousness will go before you,
and the glory of the LORD will be your rear guard.
Then you will call, and the LORD will answer;
you will cry for help, and he will say: here am I.
If you do away with the yoke of oppression,
with the pointing finger and malicious talk,
and if you spend yourselves on behalf of the hungry
and satisfy the needs of the oppressed,
then your light will rise in the darkness,
and your night will become like the noonday.
The LORD will guide you always;
he will satisfy your needs in a sun-scorched land
and will strengthen your frame.

You will be like a well-watered garden,
like a spring whose waters never fail.
Your people will rebuild the ancient ruins
and will raise up the age-old foundations;
you will be called Repairer of Broken Walls,
Restorer of Streets with Dwellings.

There's nothing like the joy I've known, when I have seen lives restored, broken people rebuilt, injustice overcome. That's what I offered myself to God for, and that's what he has done through me and all those who have offered themselves to this work.

Of course, the friendship which has sustained me more than any other is my relationship with my wonderful husband, Cliff. What a solid, solid rock he has been – and so level. I get the joys and the exhilarations, but I also get the lows. Cliff is always there, sharing them all but not overtaken by any of it, like I can be. From buying thousands of condoms and not batting an eyelid at getting them mass-delivered to our house in his name, to running me a bath when I came home from work, buying flowers for the house, praying with me, believing in me, pushing me, holding me. From cleaning out the boot of a loused-up car after I delivered a homeless man's dog into safe-keeping, to joyfully giving over all his salary to our joint project so that I could work full-time for marginalized women . . .

So perhaps it's appropriate that I finish this book with a story about Cliff.

Which is also a story about God.

Remember Lisa, the woman who came on the outing with us to the Quantock Hills? It was her birthday the same day, which already made it feel particularly special to her, but there was also something about being out in the wild of creation, with the fresh air and the wind on her face, new views and new horizons, which really affected Lisa. God started a work in her that day.

One thing I particularly remember is that at one point, Lisa happened to be at the top of a hillside, and Cliff was nearer the bottom, coming up towards us. And Lisa ran down the hill to Cliff, put her arms round him and gave him a smacking great kiss on the cheek!

This may seem a small thing, but it affected me deeply. For these women to see a man who has no interest whatsoever in what he can get from them, or how he can use them, but wants to know them as a person, is so nourishing, so healthy and, for them, so extraordinary. For someone who has used their body in the way Lisa had – who has had that body misused and abused – to have the freedom to fling her arms round a man and joyfully embrace him – well, isn't that just lovely? There's such a freedom in that, such a God-given freedom from shame and abuse and fear.

Lisa now lives just outside Bristol. She had been through One25, and was then a resident at The Well, and we had got to know each other over some years. God changed her life. What's she doing now? She's being a mum. She's with her children and she's caring for them. She is clean from drugs, her life is settled and stable, and she is loved. Praise God. I can still picture her on that exhausting, windswept day out on the hills, running down that slope with great, joyful abandon, flinging her arms around Cliff with the exhilaration of it all, and kissing him on the cheek.

One day I'll run down a wild, beautiful, windswept hill into the arms of God, and I'll give him a massive hug and smacker on the cheek. I'll say to him, 'I was there, I had a go – I made loads of mistakes, but I was available,' and he'll hold me in his arms.

Then I'll start asking him all those questions I've got . . .

Appendix: Val, in Other People's Words

Citation for Val's Honorary Degree as Doctor of Laws
Doctor of Laws
Tuesday 17 July 2018 – Orator: Professor Rona Campbell

Pro Vice-Chancellor,
    In 1777 Hannah Moore [sic], the famous Bristolian educationalist, playwright, and philanthropist wrote:

> The prevailing manners of an age depend more than we are aware, or are willing to allow, on the conduct of the women; this is one of the [principal] hinges on which the great machine of human society turns.

Bristol has been home to many pioneering women who, over the last three centuries, have fought to achieve equality for women; and social, educational and health reforms for all. Valerie Jeal, Val to those who know and have worked with her, is another great woman sprung from this tradition.
    Val was born in Northumberland but came to Bristol to train to work as a secretary. She settled here and held secretarial

posts with a variety of leading businesses in Bristol. In 1968 she joined the Department of Pathology at the University of Bristol. She was clearly very good at her job as evidenced in a fulsome acknowledgement of her organizational and secretarial skills by the editors of a book on *Oxygen Transport to Tissue* published in 1977. Val's association with books continued as she moved to a post in the University of Bristol Library. She resigned in 1991 because, at the age of 50, when many might be thinking of winding down towards retirement, Val sought a different kind of work in which she could make an immediate and lasting difference to the lives of those in our society who were, and are still, not well served by our welfare state.

Thus it was that in 1991 Val founded the Salvation Army's Candle Project for the street homeless and by her own account 'spent two years walking the streets of St Paul's in Bristol each morning, getting to know the local residents, the shop keepers, the homeless people, the heavy drinkers and the heroin addicts.' By so doing she was able to determine what services were most needed by the street homeless and then work out how the Candle Project could provide these. After five years the project was seeing sixty to a hundred people a day, mainly men, who would come in to have their basic needs for food, human companionship, and access to laundry and washing facilities met. In 2002 Val was awarded the MBE for services to homeless people in Bristol, but before that, physically and mentally burnt out by seeing so many still dying on the street, and frustrated that the service was not being used by the women selling sex on the streets, who wanted nothing to do with her, Val took a sabbatical and went to Chicago. She went to visit a project which supported women sex workers.

She was initially mistaken for the new project manager, but Pauline, one of those attending the project, quickly recognised Val's own need for care and support and took it upon herself, with the help of others, to give this visitor from the UK a very personalised tour of Chicago. In doing so Pauline restored Val's vitality and showed Val what it might be possible to achieve in Bristol.

Back in Bristol in 1995, restored after her time in Chicago, Val, equipped only with a questionnaire, chocolate and cigarettes went out to ask the women she sought to help, what they wanted. The answer came back loud and clear. What was required was a woman-only space where the women could take a break, and feel safe, so Val set about finding one. She asked for help, using all her networks, and The Movement for Faith and Justice Today who owned 125 Cheltenham Road, made a room available to her and a like-minded group of women who also wanted to help. And thus, it was, with two nuns, and practical assistance from the recently retired sexual health consultant Dorothy Milne, that the charity One25 was born.

At that stage there was no office and no money. It was Val's husband, Cliff, who paid for the 1,000 condoms a month that were delivered to their family home by a member of the postal service whom we must imagine had strong biceps and a perplexed look. In 1996, again after requests for help from Val, a van was donated to allow evening outreach on the streets; this was a yellow Ford Transit van known affectionately by the women as 'The Custard Tart'. This outreach service greatly increased the number of women with whom it was possible to have effective contact and it remains a key part of the charity's ongoing work. In 1997 the charity moved to its present site on the Grosvenor Road where it can provide all the services that the more than 200 women a year, that attend, need. Its mission remains consistent with Val's initial vision of, 'A community where all women are valued and able to live fulfilled lives', and to be fully supported if they want to build a life which doesn't involve selling sex. In the last year, of the 172 who were supported by intensive casework provided by One25, thirty-seven women made that choice, and eighty-six women gained confidence and self-worth enough to believe change is possible for them. And among a list of other impressive statistics is the fact that 139 were in stable accommodation.

Val has retired from her work at One25 but continues to volunteer at a foodbank and at a mother and toddler group in St Paul's attended by Somali women who have needs that Val is helping to meet.

For those here today who wish to make a difference to the lives of others, the example from Val is that you can do it, even if you start with no resource other than your own determination. Her example also teaches that it's important to be alongside those you wish to help, and to ask, listen and provide the help that they want.

Val is a modest, gentle person who says . . . 'It has been an enormous privilege . . . to work in the inner city with marginalised people . . . they have given far more to me than I could ever have given to them.' We are nevertheless in awe of her achievements in setting up not one, but two pioneering projects in Bristol to help the most marginalised in our city.

Pro Vice-Chancellor, I present to you, Valerie Jeal MBE, as eminently worthy of the degree of Doctor of Laws *honoris causa*.[12]

Freedom of the City of Bristol: transcript of speeches made on 7 December 2021[13]
Mayor Marvin Rees

It's incredibly special to be able to recognize amazing people and I will share – without embarrassing Val too much – that she is one of the most incredible people I've met in Bristol in my nearly 50 years in the city.

I first met Val in about '96, '97, when I came back to Bristol from university, and I was working for Tearfund and we were involved in some local outreach, and I just met Val with the beginnings of One25. (I don't know if at that time, you were still in Cheltenham Place – 125 Cheltenham Place – before moving on to Grosvenor Road. Anyway, it was all going on, it was all going on.)

Then I remember we had that very special couple of days together, when I brought – well, they were coming to visit . . . Jonathan and Thelma Nambu from Quezon City in the Philippines. I'd been to visit their work, and they were working with women that had been trafficked into the sex bars around Manila and Quezon City. They were coming to the UK, and I said I'd love to bring them to Bristol for a couple of days to spend some time with you and One25.

And it was an incredible couple of days, because it was that crossover, wasn't it, of the exploitation of women. So many of the dynamics that were happening in the Philippines were exactly the same as some of the dynamics that were happening with women over here as well. And we spent the time together, took you to Radio Bristol, did the interviews, spent time at your home having dinner together. And it was this remarkable connection of people from Asia and Europe, connecting on this common issue.

I won't share too much on some of the stories you shared in your testimony of working with the women, but I just know how much hope you've brought in to some very dark places where women have been trapped and lost, and perhaps not seen a way out. That hope has then extended into the lives of the women's children, and I also have memories of the day we went on a day trip to Longleat on a bus, and I was looking after some of the kids, and a kid in a bright yellow jacket dropped in a muddy puddle, and I had to take him and try and wipe him off! That wasn't the best moment for me, but nonetheless we did it – and just bringing some normality into the lives of the women was very special.

And something you said to me, Val, again thinking about this being twenty-odd years ago, and just how important it was – on that time, when I talked about feeling so compromised as a man, in the company of the women, when men had been the source of so much exploitation and oppression and abuse in their lives. And you said actually, they need good men around them. They need to be around men who treat them as human beings, and with respect. And actually, that was the message from Jonathan Nambu as well . . . when in the work with *Samaritana*.[14] And that has always stuck with me, that as well as advocating things, you need to embody it as well, and sometimes step into places [where] you don't always feel comfortable because there's something more important that's happening.

So it's amazing to be able to offer someone who is a good person like yourself, Freedom of the City. I'm just proud to have known you and proud to be able to call you a friend. This is a great day for us and for you. Take care.

Councillor Fabian Breckels – Labour Group

I'd like to support the granting of the Freedom of the City to Val Jeal. Val is someone I've had the pleasure of knowing for some years as we're both members of the same church – St Matthew's in Kingsdown [sic] – and someone who, like Marvin, I can call a friend.

She's a kind, calm and gentle person, so when you discover the work she's done over the years for some of Bristol's most marginalized and sidelined people, you can't help but be amazed.

After many years working at Bristol University, she moved into the voluntary sector in August '91 and founded the Salvation Army Candle Project for street homeless people in St Paul's. She remained there till '96.

After burning out in 1996, Val took a sabbatical, and she then spent some time working as a volunteer in Genesis House, Chicago, who provided housing and drop-in centres for female sex workers. Something clearly clicked for Val. It was those female sex workers in Chicago who told Val to go back to Bristol and set up a project here.

Val subsequently came home, resigned from the Candle Project and founded One25 Ltd, working with street-based female sex workers here in Bristol. The name One25 was simply the address, the property number of the first drop-in that we had.

Now the One25 project is something I'd heard of back in the '90s, so word got around about this important work, all being done without any judgement or condemnation. Clearly her work was being noticed elsewhere as well. As well as the connections Marvin has referred to, Val was later an adviser on a project for female sex workers in Thessaloniki in Greece. She was also an observer and information-gathered in Amsterdam for projects with female sex workers over there.

Following retirement from One25 in 2003 [sic], Val didn't really retire! She worked with the Home Office and the Catholic church in Bristol to set up a chain of four houses for male ex-offenders to equip them for rehabilitation.

In addition to the four men's houses, with the help of Alabaré Christian Centres she set up The Well, a six-bed [sic] house for female sex workers committed to overcoming drug and alcohol dependency and wanting to leave the sex trade. One of the residents of The Well subsequently went on to get a university degree.

Sadly, The Well closed a while ago, due to changes in funding rules, and I hope that that will be reviewed as soon as possible. In 2008, as part of One25 Ltd, Val helped set up Naomi House, a five-bed [sic] mother-and-baby unit for female sex workers. As such, it was a unit that was welcomed by Social Services, who advised on all aspects of the work, alongside the courts and the legal system.

Others have recognized Val's contribution both in Bristol and further afield, so it's time that we, Bristol City Council, caught up. In 2003 [sic] Val was awarded an MBE, and in 2018 was awarded an Honorary Doctorate of Laws by Bristol University. Our recognition of Val's tireless work, especially with our city sex workers, is long overdue.

Marvin is right. You have brought hope into some very dark places. Congratulations, Val. I can't think of a more deserving recipient for the Freedom of the City of Bristol.

Councillor Katy Grant – Green Group

Well, I have never had the privilege of meeting Val, but I have read about her life and her work. She established One25, a centre of support and protection for women leaving street sex work – often the most marginalized and isolated, and very often the victims of violence and stigma.

I was moved and impressed by what I have read, but I felt it would be much better to speak about Val through the insights of those who know her and are close to her work, so I was in touch with some of those who are working right now at One25. Anna Smith, the current CEO of One25, said this:

> Val spent her own time and energy to inspire others to support some of the most vulnerable women in the city. Women whom others do not notice, or walk by. She had times when they challenged her beyond her own perceived ability to continue, but she carried on and was inspired by them in turn. She teaches us that people can change the world with their values, their actions, and the energy they bring to others. She's changed many lives and we continue to try to do that at One25.

Another One25 colleague, Amy Sutcliffe, told me she counted herself lucky to know Val. She described Val as quiet, unassuming and humble, while being one of the most visionary and dynamic people you could hope to meet. Amy also said:

> Val is fiercely passionate about women's rights, and about giving power and a voice to women who are so often overlooked. Val has fought for justice and equality for the women that no one else [has]

listened to. She asked them what they needed, she listened to what they said, and she created a service to meet their needs – a service governed by love, free from judgement and full of hope for all.

That humility which Amy mentions is evident in Val's own words. She said, 'It was the greatest privilege of my life to work with those women, who I've grown to love and admire. It was the best job I ever had. Over the years, I've seen women take hold of their lives and be fulfilled.'

Finally, one of the women benefiting from the services of One25 has said:

> you've always made me feel accepted, beautiful and loved. Anybody can create a drop-in, but you have created a family. Most importantly, you've changed how people see us. We are no longer seen as scum. People understand that we need help getting back into society. You are responsible for this. One25 is a living, breathing family, and it loves and gives out with 125 per cent.

As the first woman in Bristol to receive the Freedom of the City, Val is yet again breaking new ground. It is not every day that a city has the chance to reward someone so deserving, who has done so much for some of its most vulnerable citizens. She's a true pioneer, and Bristol is a far better place because she calls it her home.

Councillor Lesley Alexander – Conservative Group

It is a real pleasure to be able to endorse Val for this rare honour. And Val is the rarest of them all, because, as has just been said, she is the first woman to be given this honour. The citation lists her considerable achievements, working quietly away for decades to help some of the most desperate and marginalized people in our city.

I understand Val became much more involved when she retired, so instead of seeking the quiet life, she worked even harder. Reading much of the background to Val's activities, what shines out is her commitment to these causes, and dogged determination to make a real and practical difference to those less fortunate than ourselves. This led her to set up a number of initiatives and Charitable Trusts, starting with the Salvation Army's Candle Project, which sought to give mainly homeless men in the city of St Paul's the support that they very much needed.

To help them took a number of years, to gain gradually the trust of some quite damaged individuals, which I imagine must have been emotional, challenging and demanding on Val herself. It has been rightly said that time is the most precious commodity. To give so much of it, in the cause of good works, takes a very special person. Such people are the best of us.

I know that Val has already received recognition for these services, with her MBE and Honorary Doctorate of Laws from Bristol University, but we have the authority under Local Government to confer Freedom of the City upon persons who have rendered eminent services to that place or area. Val's record of charitable services clearly qualifies for this new title, and I'm glad that we have been given the opportunity at this time to demonstrate the appreciation of her adopted city. Well done.

Councillor Jos Clark – Liberal Democrat Group

Val – before I start my speech – I don't know what you understand by being given the Freedom of the City, but you are, after today, entitled to graze your sheep on the Downs, so that is going to be a rare privilege for you! We look forward to that one!

It is a real privilege and honour to be able to support your nomination today. Your work speaks of an individual with great strength and courage, who has been able to show others your vision, enabling One25 to come into being. I heard about your work when I was on the volunteer rota for 'Loaves and Fishes'. For those who have no idea what I'm talking about, 'Loaves and Fishes' is a foodbank – and so much more – run by the Sisters of Mercy [sic], who live and work in St Paul's. (And I know Annaliese obviously through that project, and she's a marvellous lady, along with yourself.)

I was told about the work of the project One25 by other volunteers at the project. And it was clear, listening to the nuns, that your work and vision were closely aligned with their calling. What I love about your story, and I feel it is a lesson to us all – especially all councillors here today – is that you identified a need to engage with street workers and then, most importantly, you asked them what support they wanted, and then set about working with them, offering small acts of kindness, such as a warm drink or even a rose, and the services they wanted, such as a female, woman-only space.

Your work has undoubtedly made a difference to the women's lives you have touched, but your reach, and very special talents, have enabled women to make choices, and many women's lives would have been all the poorer if One25 had not been a safe place for them.

This Freedom of the City is richly deserved, and all the more important because you have quietly done all these good works for the good of the city and other people. Thank you very much indeed.[15]

The Story of One25 – Beginnings and Beyond
As told by Sister Annaliese on the One25 website

Val came with a vision and it was like something contagious which we all caught, and I think that vision was very much from God.

She came to a group that was meeting at our house, of various representatives of the different churches. She said, 'We've got to do something about these women, who's going to do it with me?' She was obedient to the promptings of God's Spirit in her heart, and we felt that. So it . . . it was a calling.

The founding members of One25 came from quite different backgrounds – some from church backgrounds, some not, and right from the beginning that was our strength.

We would draw together with the one vision we shared, to do the best we could for the women, to provide the best possible service – love, support, so that they knew that they were loved and cared for, and not alone on the streets.

I think all along, different churches have also caught the vision. Val did a lot of speaking, and I know there is one church she went to, and said, 'We need a van.' She got it clear, 'We need a van to go out to the women on the streets.' And that church got us a van!

Some would get women together who could bake cakes. Others would send money to support the project. People have been able to connect with it. And it's stirred them, it's touched people's hearts.

I think the trust that the women have shown in us has always been so humbling, really. Often sad things, but sometimes very beautiful things. And to meet another human being who shares so readily their vulnerability and brokenness, who has so very little, and yet they have so much to give. It was very much meeting Jesus in those women – Jesus who was broken.

Some of them would like to hear stories of our families. They would ask those volunteers who had children, 'How's your children?' They would want to know about another life. Being alongside the women, and them being alongside us, it just changes you completely. You can't ever look at life the same again.

I do know quite a few who have moved on with a lot of support from One25 and that's what's so heartening – not being judgemental, being alongside women where they are, and then when they realize, 'I want to get out of this', that there is that help and support there.[16]

Contact details for One25:

One25 Limited
The Grosvenor Centre
138a Grosvenor Road
St. Paul's
Bristol BS2 8YA

W: One25.org.uk
T: 0117 909 8832
E: office@one25.org.uk

Registered Charity No. 1062391
Company No. 3362644

'Val's story is one of love, tenacity, and kindness. We're honoured to continue the work that she began.'

Jenny Riley, One25 CEO

Acknowledgements

I should like to thank Jude Simpson for transforming my drafts into a publishable document. Jude has brought the whole story to life which has been both painful and joyful for me as I relived many past experiences – some printed here and others too painful to document. I am both delighted and privileged to have Jude as my co-author. Thank you, Jude.

Peter Hill has been the driving force behind the creation of this book. Peter has encouraged me over a number of years to write my story. He has guided and supported me through a long process, including participating in his Loved+Liked course in which I discovered that God not only loves me, but he likes me! I have much to thank Peter for, and he has opened a number of doors to me that would otherwise not have been there. Without Peter's friendship and support I very much doubt that this book would have been published.

Majors Melvyn and Cath Jones of Bristol Citadel were instrumental in giving me the opportunity to change my life – from the security and safety of the University Library to a journey of faith on the streets of St Paul's. Thank you.

Special thanks go to Dr Dorothy Milne, Sr Mary Donnelly and Sr Annaliese Brogden for believing that we could make a difference – together.

Friendship is a precious gift and I thank David Leonard and his late wife, Hazel, for walking with Cliff and I over many years. We shared joys, disappointments and sadness along the way. However, their love and generosity in every respect was always there for us.

My grateful thanks also go to a dear friend, Graham White, who in the early stages of my writing encouraged me to keep going. I remain grateful to Chris White for her friendship and encouragement and for joining me in One25 in the very early stages.

And, of course, my dear friend Sr Annaliese has journeyed with me for the past thirty-two years and has kept me focused. Annaliese has been a true friend – always honest and uplifting while helping me to face the reality of our lives 'on the edge'.

I am most grateful to Bishop Rachel Treweek for taking the trouble to read my drafts and to endorse the finished book. I value Bishop Rachel's endorsement as coming from a woman with the heart of God for people on the margins of our society.

Tony Collins, my literary agent, has been honest and helpful in appraising and advising during this whole process. Without Tony's help and advice in putting me in touch with Jude, I doubt that my book would have reached a publishable form.

I also thank the amazing and courageous women whose lives I have had the privilege of sharing. These include the members of staff and volunteers I worked with in the Candle Project, One25, The Well, Lazarus House and Naomi House. The female sex workers have a special place in my heart as women of courage. These women, so often shunned by society, accepted me and allowed me to share deeply in their lives. Their trust was so precious to me.

Last, but by no means least, is my husband, Cliff. Cliff has supported and encouraged me throughout our long marriage and my journey of faith. He has all too often taken a supporting role as I have ventured out in new directions. Without his love and support I could never have done the things I have done. It has been a partnership of more than fifty years, the past thirty years of which have been like living on a roller coaster. I thank you, Cliff, for all that you are and all that you have given to me in so many ways, largely unseen.

Notes

1 Edwina Gateley, *I Hear a Seed Growing* (Trabuco Canyon, CA: Source Books, 1990).

2 Gateley, *I Hear a Seed Growing*, p. xxi.

3 Nikki Jeal and Chris Salisbury, 'A health needs assessment of street-based prostitutes: Cross-sectional survey', *Journal of Public Health*, 26 (2004): pp. 147–51, https://pubmed.ncbi.nlm.nih.gov/15284317/ (accessed 20 July 2022): 10.1093/pubmed/fdh124.

4 Quote taken from: https://yellowdoor.org.uk/yellow-door-wins-top-national-award/ (accessed 8 August 2022).

5 Jon Davis, *Off the Streets: Tackling homelessness among female street-based sex workers* (London: Shelter, 2004).

6 Davis, *Off the Streets*, p. 21.

7 *Working with Sex Workers: Exiting*, UK Network of Sex Work Projects, March 2008.

8 Philip Martin, 'Human Trafficking Outpaces Drugs, Guns As World's Fastest Growing Criminal Industry', December 2010, GBH News Center; https://www.wgbh.org/news/post/human-trafficking-outpaces-drugs-guns-worlds-fastest-growing-criminal-industry (accessed 21 July 2022).

9 Now called inHope, https://www.inhope.uk (accessed 9 August 2022).

10 Verses 11 to 13 read: '"For I know the plans I have for you," declares the LORD, "plans to prosper you and not to harm you, plans to give you hope and a future. Then you will call on me and come and pray to me, and I will listen to you. You will seek me and find me when you seek me with all your heart."'

11 https://www.lovedandliked.life/ (accessed 21 July 2022).

12 See https://www.bristol.ac.uk/graduation/honorary-degrees/honorary-graduates-2018/val-jeal/ (accessed 21 July 2022).

13 Transcribed from YouTube and may contain minor inaccuracies made by the speaker on the day.

14 https://www.samaritana.org (accessed 8 August 2022).

15 Speeches transcribed by Jude Simpson from https://www.youtube.com/watch?v=4Lh_25dW2mM (accessed 21 July 2022).

16 Transcribed by Jude Simpson from https://one25.org.uk/about-us/story/ (accessed 21 July 2022).

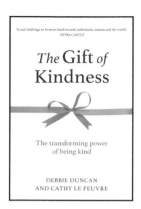

The Gift of Kindness

*The transforming power
of being kind*

*Debbie Duncan and
Cathy Le Feuvre*

Acts of kindness have the potential to make the world a happier place.
If someone is kind to you it can boost your confidence or increase
your happiness.

But kindness cannot be faked. It is much deeper than just 'being nice'.
To have real impact, kindness needs to become a lifestyle choice. We
need to actively choose to be kind every day if we want our lives to
mirror the qualities of Jesus.

Interweaving biblical and scientific insights with real life stories and
pointers for practical life application, Debbie and Cathy explore what
kindness really is and how it has the power to transform us and others.

978-1-78893-244-8

Am I Beautiful?

Breaking free from society's toxic obsession with body image

Chine McDonald

Society has one slim definition of a woman's beauty, to which most of us just don't measure up. Falling short of this standard causes pain, jealousy and self-loathing. How can we be honest about our struggles with beauty, and how do we break free from them?

Through sharing her own personal struggles with identity and critiquing society's views through the lens of the Bible, Chine shows that there truly is a path to freedom.

Christian women can be the confident, Christ-reflecting women they were created to be.

978-1-78893-292-9

The Father's Kiss

Living in the reality of God's love

Tracy Williamson

Many of us experience crippling wounds through our childhood experiences. The father heart of God longs to heal these wounds and bring joy and freedom in their place. But how do we learn to trust and love a heavenly Father when we have been hurt by our earthly fathers?

Tracy Williamson honestly shares the insights and lessons she has learnt on her own journey to freedom. With a unique mix of practical teaching, personal stories, poems, prophecies and questions for reflection, this is a life changing resource for all who carry the wounds of rejection.

Experience the reality of the Father's deep affection for you and start the adventure of a lifetime.

978-1-78078-988-0

Blood, Sweat and Jesus

The story of a Christian hospital bringing hope and healing in a Muslim community

Kerry Stillman

What is a Christian hospital doing in a remote Muslim area of Cameroon?

Kerry Stillman shares her own experiences of working as a physiotherapist in a sub-Saharan village hospital. A vivid impression of daily life is painted as the team deal with the threat of terrorism, the attitudes of local people towards western medicine, their patients' health issues, and the challenge of sensitively sharing the gospel in a different culture.

Passionate, intriguing and uplifting, this is a colourful interweaving of cultures, beliefs and the power of prayer alongside modern medicine.

978-1-78893-148-9

Be – Godly Wisdom to Live By

365 devotions for women

Fiona Castle and friends

Jesus gave us the greatest love of all. We are called not just to keep it to ourselves, but to overflow with that love to others. But how can we really do that in the busyness of our lives?

In these daily devotions, women from many walks of life share insights on scripture and practical life lessons to gently encourage you to live for Jesus, and to be more like him in your thoughts, character, and actions.

Discover godly wisdom that will help you navigate the world as a Christian woman and live out God's unique purpose for your life.

978-1-78893-239-4

Authentic

We trust you enjoyed reading this book
from Authentic. If you want to be
informed of any new titles from this author
and other releases you can sign up to the
Authentic newsletter by scanning below:

Online:
authenticmedia.co.uk

Follow us: